Breaking 80

D1355667

Breaking 80

An Amateur's Shot at Golfing
Respectability

David Godwin

YELLOW JERSEY PRESS
LONDON

Published by Yellow Jersey Press 2012

2 4 6 8 10 9 7 5 3 1

First published in Great Britain in 2012 by
Yellow Jersey Press
Random House, 20 Vauxhall Bridge Road,
London SW1V 2SA

www.vintage-books.co.uk

Addresses for companies within The Random House Group Limited can be found
at: www.randomhouse.co.uk/offices.htm

The Random House Group Limited Reg. No. 954009

A CIP catalogue record for this book
is available from the British Library

ISBN 9780224082860

The Random House Group Limited supports The Forest Stewardship Council
(FSC®), the leading international forest certification organisation. Our books
carrying the FSC label are printed on FSC® certified paper. FSC is the only forest
certification scheme endorsed by the leading environmental organisations,
including Greenpeace. Our paper procurement policy can be found at
www.randomhouse.co.uk/environment

Typeset in Bembo by Palimpsest Book Production Limited,
Falkirk, Stirlingshire
Printed and bound by CPI Group (UK) Ltd, Croydon, CR0 4YY

For Heather.

Who has always been wary of golf but finished up
cheering Rory McIlroy's US Open victory
long after I had gone to bed.

Contents

Contents

This is a story of a journey, though it turned out not to be the journey I thought it would be.

Introduction
The Packer Tournament

6.45 a.m. on a late March morning in 2008 and I'm standing outside Aldeburgh Golf Club. The clubhouse is locked and the car park deserted. It is cold and blustery with dark clouds gathering to the west. The forecast is rain.

I have been told that I should practise before I play, and that is why I have arrived an hour and a half before the match is scheduled to begin. I am slightly alarmed that no one else has found it necessary to be here this early but undeterred I cross the road to the practice ground and hit balls with a five iron for twenty minutes or so until it starts to rain. By now the clubhouse is open so I order a coffee and wait for the others to arrive. Today is the day of the Packer Rejects Golf Tournament – an invitational event set up over thirty years ago. It is the first time I have been invited. It is my first competition. I am sixty. I have no handicap. I am a bag of nerves.

The Packer Rejects Tournament was dreamt up in 1976 by a friend, Simon de Galleani, and his brother-in-law, David. Originally it was intended as a cricket tournament, set for a summer day in 1977. The twenty-two players arrived but that day it rained and rained and the match was cancelled. Instead they headed for Aldeburgh Golf Club which has perfect drainage and a golf tournament was born.

Simon decides who plays with whom and what handicaps we should have if we don't have official ones. By eight o'clock all twenty-two of us have arrived. We gather round. We are all men, some I know, and one or two I have played with before, but for the most part they are strangers and I have no idea how good they are. My nervous tension increases.

Simon explains that in the morning we are to play two-ball foursomes, which involve two teams of two players − hence foursomes − with each player taking it in turns to play a shot − hence two balls. I have never played golf in a team before. The afternoon is to be taken up with a singles match. Every man for himself. For the morning session Simon, somewhat bravely and very kindly as I am the new boy, pairs himself with me. We are the first foursome to go out and I have to drive off in front of everybody.

We start on the thirteenth. Probably the first thing I learnt is that golf clubs have masses of rules. Most of these seem to cover which hole you are supposed to start on. Common sense suggests that this should be the first, but apparently that is too simple.

I can see the thirteenth green from the tee and the fairway runs down to a ridge with gorse on either side. I had played here with Simon several months earlier − I suspect he was checking that I had some inkling of how to play – and on that occasion my drive had finished up on the neighbouring fairway to my right, probably the worst slice I had ever played. I try to blot out that memory as I get out my three wood, place the tee in the ground, the ball on the tee, and have a couple of practice swings. I take a deep breath. The ball sweeps into the air and races away down the fairway. Straight. We stride off.

There are still heavy grey clouds and the wind is getting up but at least the rain has stopped. Throughout the round I am so nervous about playing badly that I take no risks, lamely hitting the ball down the fairway, avoiding the bunkers. Simon, being a stronger player, takes a few chances and once or twice the ball finishes up in the gorse but we get to the end with a score of ninety. I have not disgraced myself.

As we sit eating lunch by the large windows facing the course we watch the weather close in. I am beginning to relax but decide not to drink any wine or beer. Instead I order two Rock Shandies, a curious non-alcoholic drink of lemonade and angostura bitters and some mysterious extras that vary from club to club. It is a golfer's drink, invented in colonial Africa. I once tried to order it in a pub in Padstow and got a very strange look. By now it is raining so heavily that I head back to the car to get my rain gear – waterproof trousers, cap, anorak, towels and an umbrella. Plus of course a special cover for the golf bag to keep the clubs dry. Although I am a novice I have come prepared.

Suitably dressed I arrive at the tee to begin my singles match. I am teamed with Ant, one of the original competitors from 1977. We start at the first, at last, and my drive is fine. My second is a bit short but by the time I reach the green, I am desperate for a pee. I have waterproof trousers over my ordinary trousers and no zip in the waterproofs. I know I have to get the ball into the hole before I can disappear into the gorse. By now the rain is serious, which is making me even more desperate to pee. I putt quickly, short, putt again, too long. I miss back and eventually get down in four putts. I hurriedly make for the gorse.

The rain gets worse and as we reach the sixth hole Simon arrives to ask us if we want to stop, given the conditions. Part of me is longing to give up, but I feel too new to offer an opinion. I take my lead from Ant.

'Oh no,' Ant says gamely, 'we want to keep going.' I nod in agreement.

The rain is seeping down my back; my glasses are covered in water giving a strange blurry effect as I try to work out where I want my ball to go on the fairway. I have been told that visualisation is very important to the success of a golf shot. We stumble on. I lose balls in the gorse, miss shots, get caught in bunkers and by the time we reach the last few holes the wind is so strong I can barely hit the ball any distance at all. I drive a reasonable tee shot on the last hole but eventually when I reach where I think it landed, to my absolute dismay there is no sign of it. We wander up and down the fairway and eventually agree the ball has probably disappeared down a rabbit hole. It seems a suitable way to end what has turned into an Alice-in-Wonderland round.

Afterwards I drive a few miles north up the coast to Southwold where I am staying, feeling cold, miserable and exhausted. Within the hour, after a hot bath, I am back on the A12 for the prize-giving. It is 6.15 in the evening. There are three prizes – for the best teams, for the best rounds, and for the senior player of the year. I am not among the winners. During the course of the presentation I desperately try to work out where it has all gone wrong. The conditions were atrocious, but it was the same for everybody. The winners talk confidently of punching the ball into the wind. Later that night I search through the indexes of my golf books looking for tips on how to punch the ball.

I am determined never to play so badly again. The next Packer is set for the following September. With luck the weather might be better then. I have eighteen months.

Not long after the Aldeburgh debacle I was having lunch with a publisher who also plays golf. She asked me if I had ever scored eighty. I laughed. Eighty – it had such a mythical ring. I knew this was the crucial figure that separated the men from the boys. Famously Tiger Woods had passed it when he was seven. Here was I, a sixty-year-old man, how could I possibly get that much better? My singles score that afternoon in Aldeburgh was over one hundred. It seemed a vainglorious challenge, but of course irresistible. My head swam and before I collected myself I found myself saying 'Let me try. To win and score eighty.' This book is an account of my attempt to break eighty and win the Packer Rejects Championship. Could a middle-aged weekend golfer with a high handicap ever really improve? I was about to find out.

I

Southwold

My interest in golf began with a visit to the doctor. In June 2007 I had a urinary infection. At the time we were on holiday in Southwold, the home of Adnams beer. The brewery itself is in the centre of the town. We have a small cottage a few yards from the brewery in one direction and the beach in the other. It is not much bigger than a beach hut.

The GP there did a number of tests. I returned to the surgery a week later expecting a course of antibiotics. He came straight to the point.

'Do you know you have type two diabetes?'

Diabetes – that sounded serious. I remembered that my father had suffered from it but he had refused to talk about it, one of the many subjects he refused to talk about. He had chosen to ignore the whole business. The doctor explained that I would have to change my diet and lose weight.

I went back to the cottage and discussed the whole thing with Heather, my wife.

'No more Waitrose trifles for you,' she said firmly and

I thought just a bit too gleefully, 'and you need lots of exercise. You're too fat.'

I was, yes. Fourteen stone. As a young man I had been skinny and never worried about weight, but over the years I had accumulated a neat but substantial paunch. I had no waist and my shirts felt uncomfortably tight. Something had to be done. I decided to go for a wander across the local common to think what I should do. I am not a cyclist. I have played tennis, though erratically. I used to play cricket but clearly I was now too old for that, and anyway it is too seasonal. As I walked across the common and alongside the golf course I had to stop to let a golfer drive over the footpath. An idea began to form.

I had played golf as a boy. I had some clubs – they had been my father's – and I could play on my own which meant I could exercise on a regular basis. There are courses all over the place. So golf it was. I went home and told Heather.

'Oh no!' she said. 'You can't. Golf is *awful*. You hate golfers.'

'You mustn't confuse golf with golfers,' I said. 'Bryan plays golf and he's nice.'

'He is the exception,' she said.

'OK. Let's ask him and Lesley up and I can play with him.'

Bryan and Lesley are friends from St Albans where we live. I knew I had a major job to persuade Heather of the virtues of golf. Bryan was important but I wondered if he would be enough, so before long I was leaving the works of John Updike around the house hoping she would get the message. Heather has always been vulnerable to a good book, thank God, and Updike is probably the best writer on golf. If that failed, I was also beginning to investigate the world of art, knowing as I did that Ben Nicholson, the St Ives artist, was a fanatical golfer. So far, though, that was only a back-up.

Bryan is a Glaswegian and a serious scientist – a professor, a fellow of the Royal College of Pathologists, head of a cancer genomics group and head of an oncology laboratory. One evening we were chatting about haircuts, as men do, and he said he'd only ever use the local barber, would never pay more than a fiver for a haircut and certainly wouldn't *ever* use anyone in London – 'not those teasy weasies!' The name stuck. TW he became.

On the day of our first game together I used my father's old clubs. It was an odd feeling. I still have them – though I don't use them any more – and looking at them recently made me wonder what other things I have of his. There are no books – I have no memory of him reading anything except a paper – in fact I can't associate him with any objects. All the furniture in the house was my mother's; he had no special things, except perhaps a cricket bat that was signed by fellow members of his RAF team which he won at Lord's in 1948. I found it recently, half rotten at the bottom of the garden shed.

I had not yet committed sufficiently to this new game to splash out on expensive gear.

TW had a serious set of clubs. And a trolley. I carried my own clubs. The golf course has nine greens but each hole has two different tees making it an eighteen-hole course. As with Aldeburgh there is a lot of gorse. And there is wind. The fairways are narrow and I struggled to give TW a decent game. He won, as expected, but I was beginning to get the feel of the game: the difference between clubs and the way the greens worked. TW explained the rules and procedures, what the blue markers in the middle of the fairway meant – 150 yards to the green – and when the flag on the green can be removed from the hole – when you are putting – and so on. It was clear that there were a lot of rules and conventions.

That night we all went out for supper at the Nelson, a pub just round the corner from the cottage. There was a lot of golf talk. Heather asked TW if I was any good. He was characteristically generous and encouraged me to keep playing and the conversation drifted on. We started to talk about the kind of things that made us happy. TW didn't hesitate for a second, 'Beating David at golf.' In fact he said it was an exquisite pleasure. I remember his exact words and felt something in the air change. That was the moment that improving my game became *really* important.

The following weekend I was back in Southwold. It was my birthday and Heather, by now having admitted defeat – I am sure reading Updike did the trick – said she would buy me a new set of golf clubs as there was no way I could make much progress with the old ones. Also it seemed too odd for a man in his sixties to be using his dad's clubs. We set off for the golf club and I explained to Brian, the pro, that I needed a new set of inexpensive clubs that would do the job. I walked out with a brand new set of clubs, a pair of shoes, a trolley and a series of lessons, all for just over £150.

Brian and I met the next day for lesson number one. The practice area in Southwold is below the clubhouse on land drained from the marsh which in turn stretches down to the harbour and the river Blyth beyond. Brian set me up, sorted out my grip and explained the basic principles. I started hitting five irons down towards the flag and the balls flew to and fro, some wide, some short, none too long. He took me through all the clubs and I learnt the difference between wedges and fairway woods and then we went back to the putting green alongside the clubhouse. He showed me how to hold the putter and how to line up my putts. He stressed I was never to move my head, that was the surest way to send the ball wide of the hole.

Every afternoon I paid my green fee – it was cheaper after one o'clock. Brian's comments went round and round in my head as I marched up and down the fairways. I began to feel a kind of confidence; the ball was beginning to do what I wanted. So after a few weeks I called TW and asked him if he fancied another game. We agreed to play at Harpenden, a few miles north of St Albans, where he was a member. I was absolutely fired up with my new clubs, and keen to give him a run for his money. It worked. Within moments I was racing ahead, hole after hole. In fact, I think I was just having a lucky day but I succeeded in beating him by as much as he had beaten me four weeks earlier. Progress.

It was a fluke that I beat TW – he was clearly a better player than me. I knew by now that I had to start to play properly. The first thing was to join a club and perhaps get a handicap. Southwold seemed the perfect place to start as we spend most weekends there. I went into the clubhouse to meet Peter, the secretary. Peter explained I needed a sponsor to become a member of the club.

However, as I told him I did not know anyone in Southwold who played golf, he gave me a funny look and then generously waived that restriction. I signed the forms, paid the fees and I was a member. I had no interest in the clubhouse, which was just as well as it was rarely open. It was the golf that I was there for. I played and played day in and day out.

The public has rights all over the course, so crossing it can be perilous both for golfers and walkers. Bicycles suddenly appear out of the gorse and dog walkers are everywhere. I once came across a family having a picnic in one of the bunkers and have often found people lying on their backs sunbathing on the fairways. But I began to learn the game properly, no small talk, just putting, chipping and learning the language of golf whatever the weather. I was losing weight and getting fitter.

However, there was a dark side, well grey really, as I began to realise that not everyone loved golf as I now did. People out with their dogs would obstinately walk down the fairway towards me as I waited to play my shots. I was patient as they walked past. There was even an incident when someone poured petrol on one of the greens and completely killed the grass. Clearly there was some serious friction between the golfers and the non-golfers, and I began to find myself defending the golfers, even to Heather. She regularly walked across the common with Jock our Jack Russell and could never work out where the balls were coming from. I took her over the whole course to show her where the tee boxes were and which tee was for which green, but she had no feel for the geography of golf.

Having sharpened up my basic shots, I needed to find some golfing allies. I started seeking out friends who played golf and this is initially what led me to Simon and the Packer Rejects. We both live in St Albans and he had heard from another friend that I was becoming embroiled in the golf circus.

We met and played at his local course in Radlett, and during the course of the game he explained how the Rejects had been set up. He asked me if I would like to join them, and hence I found myself in Aldeburgh on that rainy day in March.

After the Packer Tournament it was clear I had to make some serious plans if I were genuinely to improve. I needed a handicap. This was suddenly made more urgent when I was asked by the writer Tim O'Grady to join a group of golfers in Valencia. I should explain that I am a literary agent. I represent writers and my job is to sell their books and to handle their literary affairs around the world. Tim is one of my clients. He is also an extremely good golfer. He explained I needed a handicap before I could play. I needed to play three rounds with someone to mark my card, as golfers would say, basically to keep my score. The worse you are the higher your handicap. This allows players of different skill to play against one another. So if I played Tiger Woods, for example, he would give me a number of shots. (In my case I would probably need a hundred shots to compete evenly but the maximum handicap is twenty-eight.) It is like being given a head start for a race. In this way golf is a generous and thoughtful game.

It was now April, just a month after the Packer match, and the Valencia match was in May. I needed to train like never before. I approached Brian the pro to see if he would mark my card. It was going to be expensive – Brian's time needed to be paid for – but Brian didn't have the time anyway so he suggested that I talk to Peter, the secretary of the golf club.

'That's fine,' said Peter, 'next Tuesday at twelve.'

I was on the putting green a good hour before we met, eager to impress. After a while Peter came out with a small bag of clubs slung over his shoulder, and we walked to the first tee.

'Off you go,' he said. The first hole is rather confusing. It looks shorter than it is and it has bunkers all around the green so the shot has to go high to reach it. Basically a decent shot from the tee should put you on the green. There is gorse on both sides and a path runs in front of the bunkers. We waited till a family went past with two dogs and a buggy. My first shot went over to the right, a slice, but it was safe. He drove on to the green. I walked up, played an eight iron on to the green, two putts for a four. A good start. We went through the gorse to the second tee.

This is the longest hole on the course. The town sewage works is on the left so there is a distinctive and not altogether pleasant smell as you prepare to drive down the fairway. I drove straight, hit two more shots up to the ridge guarding the green, then one over the ridge and down in six. Every hole has a par, which is the number of shots a good player would take to get the ball into the hole on the green. Par also assumes you need two putts on every hole, and never more than two. In this instance the second hole has a par of five; I scored a six which is one over par – a bogey. I asked Peter why it was called that but he had no idea. The third turns back to the clubhouse. This is a par four which I did in six.

'OK, let's go and have a drink,' said Peter.

We walked back and he asked me casually what handicap I thought I should have. I said I thought twenty was pretty fair. We reached the clubhouse, and he held the door open for me and said that he thought twenty was perfect. I bought him a pint. I walked home and explained to Heather that I now had an official handicap. I tried to explain to Heather how all this worked but I could feel her attention wandering. Anyway, I was off to Spain.

I caught a flight to Valencia to join a group of twenty men. We met at the hotel. I was the only one in a single room. I had sworn never to share a room with another man after years of being cooped up in dormitories at boarding school. We met for dinner. Most of the men were from Northern Ireland and all knew each other, in fact most were related to each other, and there was a large man at the end of the table, whom I later found out was Mike, telling jokes and generally being the man of the moment. I was a bit nervous so kept quiet. As the meal progressed the conversation turned to golf and handicaps.

'What is yours?' Mike asked, turning to me.

Eager to join in with the banter I told them the story of how I had been awarded my handicap. I thought it would at least make them laugh. Mike asked to see my certificate. I got it out of my jacket pocket rather proudly and passed it down the table. Mike held it up to the light.

'Well you know what this is worth,' and he proceeded to tear it to pieces, dropping them all on the floor.

Everyone fell about laughing.

I wondered if this meant I would have to go home without playing. Would I be reported to the golf authorities, whoever they were? Suddenly I had some vague memory of the Royal and Ancient and I remembered the rule book that TW had often consulted. Perhaps my golf career was over, branded as a cheat and a fake.

Tim turned to me and said, 'Don't worry. We'll just go on with your handicap as is. Mike is just winding you up. Come on, let's go to the bar.'

We did, and in desperation I bought everyone a drink and tried to be sociable and jolly. It was quite hard.

The course was outside Valencia and overlooked by a parador. It ran alongside the sea and meandered through olive groves. A far cry from the windswept landscape of the Suffolk coast. I was selected to play with Tim. He drove off first and without a second thought strode off down the fairway. Welcome to competitive golf. I struggled behind making a dismal score well over my handicap, totting up a miserable amount of points, placing me well down on the leader board. Tim was way up on the top.

The day was extremely hot and most of my competitors looked alarmingly red, having refused to use any sun cream, and insisted on wearing shorts. I went off to have a swim and the next two days went much as the first. On the final day I was in the first pair out – the losers, in fact – and finished bottom with a total of fifty-two points. This had to be the worst, so I could only get better. I flew home and was soon back at the drawing board in Southwold.

I retreated into solitary golf with the dog as my only companion. I had also taken to walking him along the golf course, usually on the lookout for balls. I often took a golf club with me. One rainy Thursday I was in gumboots with a golf club, a ball and Jock. I was on the fairway of the sixth which adjoins the cricket field and I gently knocked a ball forward with my eight iron. Before I knew it a stout man was striding towards me across not one but two fairways.

'I see you are playing golf,' he panted when he reached me.

'Well I'm really just walking my dog,' I explained.

'Have you paid a green fee?'

I explained that I hadn't.

'I think you should go now to the clubhouse and pay a green fee.'

He pointed back to the clubhouse. I explained perfectly calmly that I was simply walking my dog, yes I had a golf club with me and a golf ball but I was walking *away* from the green. He was not persuaded so I delivered my trump card and told him I was actually a member and in fact had a perfect right to play even though I was not in fact playing. He looked me up and down.

'You should be ashamed of yourself, you're wearing jeans,' he said as he turned and made his way back across the fairway to his abandoned clubs.

Is this the club golfer, I wondered? Everyone I know thought golfers were a cheerless bunch and this seemed pretty convincing proof of how right they were. I became fearful of the world I was beginning to enter.

It was not that much later that I was out playing on my own, which at that time under the rules of the golf soviet – the Royal and Ancient, which is housed alongside the eighteenth green at St Andrews and is responsible for all the golf rules the world over – meant I had no status so could be disregarded by everyone playing on the course. It was a quiet evening. I had played three holes and reached the green of the fourth when suddenly I heard voices and a man and a woman went past me on the adjoining fairway of the next hole. They had cut in front of me. I reached the tee and watched them making their way down my fairway, yes mine. I waited and then drove. I had decided I would catch them up, which I did after a couple of holes.

'Excuse me, but I think you cut in front of me on the fifth,' I said to the man who was just leaving the green.

'Oh I don't think so,' said the woman to my left, butting in.

'Oh yes you did, I was just leaving the green and you jumped in front of me. You went from the first to the fifth.'

'Are you on your own?' she asked.

'Yes.'

'Well then you have no status and we can push in front of you if we want to.'

'I'm sure the rules don't let you push in front of people,' I said rather grandly, 'I'm a member here too and I think you owe me an apology.'

'Rules are rules,' she said.

She was gone, striding up the fairway, a ship in full sail. My moment had gone. I wandered back to my car and drove home.

Was this ghastly woman the true golfer and I just a wishy-washy interloper? Perhaps golf was not for me after all. I resigned from the Southwold Golf Club. I loved the golf but not the golfers. As usual I felt the odd one out and I wondered if I would ever find a golf club where I would feel at home. I thought I would try to join TW's club in Harpenden. However, in the back of my mind I was beginning to wonder if *I* was the problem.

2

Harpenden

TW gave me the forms and I applied to join Harpenden Golf Club. After ten days the secretary phoned and asked me to go in for an interview. Before I set off, to my shame, I put on a tie, which I found at the back of my drawer. There were three to interview me.

'Tell us a bit about yourself,' the captain said.

I rambled on about being a literary agent but this was clearly not the time or place to get into the intricacies of e-book rights, so they asked me about my previous membership in Southwold. I had a momentary panic and wondered if there was some system whereby clubs could warn each other of unclubability, or if a member had committed some particular gross act on the golf course, but there were no knowing winks and it seemed they had no previous knowledge so I simply mentioned I wanted a more challenging course. This appeared to be the answer they wanted.

'You seem fine, just behave yourself on the course and use the bar as much as possible. But you have to have a round with Frank first and if he is happy then you're in.'

'Thank you,' I said. I did not quite say 'sir', but very nearly.

Frank and I arranged to meet the following Friday. Unfortunately the week before the game was given over to a long and bruising set of e-mails, phone calls and arguments between me and a publisher about a writer who was keen to leave them and move on. He was halfway through a three-book contract but the writer and I both felt the relationship was really in trouble – there were lots of arguments about changing the ending of his book, as they wanted a different version to the one he had given them – so I told them we were going to break the contract and leave. It was hard to know if they wanted him to stay or would be relieved if he went. They said they would ring on the Friday afternoon with their response. They had my mobile number, but of course that afternoon I would be playing my key round with Frank and the rules are perfectly clear, no phones on the course. I remembered the unsolicited advice from that woman in Southwold – that rules are rules.

I decided to play it straight and explained the problem to Frank. Rather to my surprise he seemed fine and we set off. The game was going well, no phone interruptions until we reached the sixteenth green. I was about to putt when my phone went off. I had to take the call, and before I knew it I was trying to putt with one hand and hold the phone with the other. The phone call was bad news – the publisher refused to accept my proposals, the writer had to stay. For a moment it looked as if I had lost both the argument and my chance to join Harpenden Golf Club.

As I shot off down the fairway Frank began quizzing me about the whole business. We talked about it down the remaining three fairways. I explained to him that I had been a publisher for many years then moved into agenting, and I now represented over a hundred writers. He was interested to know if there were any golf writers among them, or better still major personalities or celebrities who could come along to the golf dinners they held every month. I represent some celebrities and some golfers, but I couldn't think of one who combined golf and celebrity in quite the way that he was after. Again I thought I may have blown it but when we reached the eighteenth we putted out and shook hands. 'You are in,' he said. I had a new home. I explained all this to Heather that night saying it was a new start and I was sure this club would work better than Southwold. She gave me an odd look.

If I was ever to break eighty I needed a clear understanding of the strengths and weaknesses of my game. So I decided I should make an accurate record of every round, what club I used and crucially how many putts I took on every hole. It would be easier to do this if I played on my own. I knew TW would be horrified to see such obsessional behaviour. I started on a beautiful, but windy, Saturday afternoon. I set off to Harpenden, or Hammonds End as it should be called to distinguish it from the other course on Harpenden Common.

Hammonds End was a breakaway from the latter, though no one in the clubhouse could quite tell me why.

Hammonds End is a typical parkland course with twelve holes on one side of a road, and six holes on the other. The first three holes go up and down and the fourth moves away past the rugby club, and the sixth finishes up at the far corner of the course before coming back to the clubhouse. The twelfth runs adjacent to the road with the green finishing right by the first tee. The thirteenth tee is alongside the clubhouse and is the first of the last six holes. The tee box is above the green and the fairway runs downhill with bunkers protecting the green; this and the remaining holes are the best of the course. The fourteenth goes off towards farmland, the fifteenth swinging right, then a short hole before the seventeenth coming home with a difficult drive and the fairway angled so the ball runs down the slope to the grass on the right and the green is protected by a line of trees. The last hole has a high tee, a dip and a slope and a wood on the right which acts like a magnet for all wayward drives. There are more balls in there than plants.

Hammonds End does not have a policy of booking tee times but instead has an elaborate system of starting at different times at the thirteenth, near the clubhouse, or the first, which often means when you arrive at the thirteenth you meet a number of players waiting to go off, while the first is empty. Puzzling.

It seemed quiet as I set off from the first. Not a great start as I noted a seven on my card, then I realised there were a number of people in front, a four-ball, elderly, with power trolleys, much criss-crossing from one fairway to another. I was held up and very soon another four-ball appeared in my wake. I was not entirely clear about the status of a single player. I had a sinking feeling there was trouble ahead but I optimistically hoped there would be local rules covering it. By the time I reached the third tee, they were on the green behind me. I was trapped with the elderlies behind and in front. A man with the Harpenden golf V-neck sweater came towards me.

'We're going through, hope that's OK.'

I explained that I was delayed by the people in front who were very slow and that I was not the problem. He was not convinced. I was simply a single player, with no status. I smiled and said fine, inwardly raging of course but I kept it under control. I thought instead I would trek across the eighteenth fairway to the practice ground. On the way I asked another member what the rule was exactly, as I vaguely remembered that recently the single player had been given status by the R and A. The member explained that this did not apply to Harpenden, it had a special local rule which maintained the status quo. Rather appropriate, I thought, as I walked off.

For Harpenden, clubability is everything: they want you to play with others, yes it takes longer, but what does that matter as one chats away ambling down the fairway? I began to wonder if I was taking all this a little too seriously.

I reached the practice ground and remembered that all the books not only tell you to record every shot but also to find out how far exactly you hit the ball with each club. It was very windy. I diligently went through all my clubs – I must have been there for over two hours

– and tried to work out the distances, but of course all the books assume you hit the ball straight and you can simply average out the distance.

No such luck. The balls seem to be splayed all over the fairway and suspiciously all the clubs over a five – I had a three and a four iron – seemed to carry roughly the same distance. And of course you can never remember which club hit which ball. Maybe I should invent different coloured balls with numbers on them. And a microchip in them so I could find all those wayward drives into the bushes. But my three wood, shorter than a driver but with a more angled head, could go further. I reckoned on a still day 180 yards, but it was a disaster in the wind. I tried to hit the ball lower under the wind but I had no idea what I was doing. I remembered that terrible afternoon in the wind at the Packer championship.

I realised I would get nowhere without proper lessons, but before I started with Peter – the professional there – I decided to go back to Brian in Southwold. There seemed to be so many things I needed to understand about golf and I was beginning to be bewildered by the whole issue of clubs, technique, and rules. I was also heading for my next birthday and I could feel some panic.

Brian had been working at Southwold as their pro for over thirty years. When I arrived I parked in the corner of the car park a little nervous of seeing my old adversaries, but there was no sign of them or even Peter the secretary. We agreed to play a round. We set off. My drive with a five iron skidded to the left under a tree. 'Take your punishment,' said Brian as I knocked the ball sideways, then a chip, two putts – a five on a par three. Eighty seemed a very distant prospect. I explained my project to Brian and his first comment was that I would never do it as long as I was thinking about it as I played. Little did I know then how right he would prove to be.

Brian explained as we wandered down the fairways that golf was essentially a mental game. I could hardly believe it, not another thing to worry about. It was bad enough trying to control my arms, my wrists, shoulders, legs, and now the mind. I wondered how on earth I could train my mind to be calm, not to fret over every shot, but Brian explained I had to have a routine, and that the routine itself would still the mind. As I approached the ball I should stop talking and concentrate. I should examine the lie, work out how far I was from the hole using the blue markers, select a club, make two practice swings, visualise where the ball was going to land then concentrate purely on the ball with everything else banished from my brain. Then hit with my body still and composed. As I lifted my head I would see the ball arching its way through the air towards the target.

Now with all this in mind I played a number of holes, yes a little better at first but everything seemed to collapse as soon as I reached the green. You are only supposed to take two putts on every green but I seemed to be taking a lot more. I rarely hit the ball straight and often either too long or too short. At the sixth, Brian, who had been watching me pretty closely on all the greens so far, took me to one side as I lined up my putts.

'You're a hopeless putter, your alignment is completely wrong – you have no chance of holing these putts.'

Tell me about it. He explained how I had to stand square to the ball, keeping the ball in the middle. My stance was rather that of a cricket player with all my weight on the front foot. So I did as he suggested on the remaining three holes and gradually the ball got closer to the hole; but not in.

We returned to the clubhouse, a simple wooden building perched above the tennis courts. We sat outside and had a drink. Brian was in a reflective mood. He wondered out loud whether he had been there too long. We talked about the relationship between the professional and the club members. He felt, perfectly rightly, that the members should buy the clubs and balls from the pro shop but they rarely do these days with internet deals everywhere. Also the members are older and keen to save their cash, again perfectly understandable.

The golf course itself seemed precarious, unable to resolve its relationship with the town – keen to keep its distance, wary of the weekenders and holidaymakers, determined to keep its dress code but forced to recognise that the battle is lost, and that people do want to play in trainers. I walked home across the golf course with the sun dipping in the west sending shadows across the fairway. It was beautiful. There were lots of people walking their dogs along and across the fairways – it was nice to see a golf course used, not fenced in against intruders.

I returned to Hertfordshire and a new programme of lessons began. It started with a cup of coffee with Peter in the clubhouse and I explained my plans. Peter was wonderfully optimistic. He is a modern pro. He used to play on the circuit, as they call it; he has read all the books and studied the psychology of golf. I felt in terrific hands and we set to work. The first lesson was about balance. I swung my six iron and he explained that I had no chance of hitting my shots accurately if my balance was so hopeless. I kept moving my feet at the end of the swing, tipping and twisting one way or another. Watching amateurs play I had always noticed how their bodies tip and twist and overbalance, whereas good players and professionals are wonderfully still. First, Peter told me to stand still on just one foot then another, which I did reasonably well. Then he told me to do it with my eyes closed. It seemed impossible. He then sent me away to practise. The next day I was standing on the railway platform. I remembered Peter's instruction so I stood like a heron elegantly perched on one foot, before hopping on to the other. The men beside me read their papers. No one gave me a second look.

By the time of the second lesson I had begun to master the art of balance. This next lesson was about the circle, as Peter called it. He explained how the club should move through a perfect plane touching the ground where the ball sat before circling around my left shoulder. He explained that length should be a product of the rhythm of the shot. So circle it was, the club finished where it had started. It seemed to work and I was beginning to understand the physics of the game.

With renewed enthusiasm I went out first thing every morning that week, and my notebook filled up with details of every shot as I made my way round the course.

I usually set off around six o'clock, and reached the thirteenth at about eight. If I got there before then it was fine, there was no one there and I could complete my round, but if I was late there was usually a set of men already on the tee. I tried to explain that I had already played twelve holes but they clearly thought I was simply trying to barge in front of them and they would send me back to the first. At that point I usually gave up, drove home and went to work, and no one was any the wiser that I had already been up for several hours.

The following weekend I went out with TW. I had so much in my head – circles, and balance – but I went round in a solid ninety shots. Not great, too many putts. As we went round the course we talked about his daughter's wedding in St Andrews at the end of June. He suggested we went up a few days early and played some golf. I was thrilled.

We took the flight to Edinburgh and hired a car and drove to St Andrews. We stayed at Russett's Hotel and our rooms overlooked the eighteenth green on the Old Course. Perfect.

The Old Course is the most important golf course in the world. It was here that golf began and all the original Open Championships were played here, usually won by a whole set of Scottish golfers. The Royal and Ancient Clubhouse stands beside the eighteenth green, a large grey building that dominates the whole course. I learnt from TW that in fact the course itself was owned by the local council which had made an arrangement with the R and A that, unless there were exceptional circumstances, there should be no golf on Sundays and people from the town would be free to walk the course.

The wedding was on the Saturday but we had Friday to play golf. In the morning we went over to Crail which is a historic course, no trees, double greens, the first traditional course I had ever come across. And wind. It runs alongside the sea and on the fifth you have to drive over the beach. I crashed my drive towards the green and found the ball heading out to sea. No matter, it was the perfect practice for the competition that afternoon.

TW had chosen to play on the Eden course, one of seven courses at St Andrews, and we assembled at the clubhouse. There were fifteen of us and TW told us who was playing with whom. Golf is played in groups of never more then four. I was in a four comprising David, an ex-publisher and keen golfer, the bridegroom's father and his son, Sam, both Irish, and myself. Sam I think had never played before, whereas the rest of us were roughly of the same standard. I was the only one with a handicap so TW decided whoever had the lowest score would win. I thought back to my disastrous days in Spain and tried to gather up everything I had learnt.

We set off down the first. Everything was fine till we reached the green. Usually as the ball nears the hole, shots become easier as the distance between the ball and the hole decreases. Sam's singular skill was to reverse this process so as he neared the hole he would usually overhit the shot so the ball was further from the hole than before, sometimes running off the green entirely. I had never seen the sequence of putt, wedge, putt, wedge, putt before.

The ball regularly shot from one edge of the green not simply to the other side but often back to the fairway or to the fairway beyond the green. There were peals of laughter as the ball ricocheted around, but Sam was undeterred and carried on till the ball plopped in the hole. He was both wonderfully cheery and distracting. I thought I was doing much better than I was. I added up my score as I reached the tenth. Forty-nine shots over the first nine holes and I realised I had no chance of winning. This was ridiculous so I decided to pull myself together and to really concentrate. It worked.

The tenth is a short hole hitting over a small lake to the green. Suddenly I had found my focus, and my drive landed on the green. So far in the round I had hit no tee shots which reached the green, let alone as close to the pin as this was. I was jolted into action. It was probably just luck but it felt like success. All my concentration was now on the ball, and my interest in Sam's exploits drifted away. Once I reached the green I carefully examined the route from the ball to the hole, and I worked out the ball would drift to the left. I kept my head down and the putt almost made it but I was down in three, a par. It was an incredible feeling, a kind of elation and I raced through the next holes.

Driving down the fairway and dropping the putts hole after hole, my guardian angel was with me as I came to the last hole. It is a tricky hole with a wall and bushes protecting it. I drove to the left into the rough. I could not see the hole but I knew it was over a hundred yards just beyond the wall. My choice was either to hit the ball back to the fairway then play safely on to the green, or to go for it. I picked up my wedge, visualised my ball on the green and struck.

The ball went up over the wall. I dropped my club and raced round to see where it had landed. It was on the green not far from the pin. I collected my clubs and waited for the rest of my colleagues to reach me before missing the putt, but I was down in four. I added up my score for the back nine. I had made thirty-nine, the best nine holes I had ever played. We went into the clubhouse and waited for everyone to finish. We passed the cards to TW. He announced the winner with an eighty-eight. It was me. The Wedding Cup was mine. He presented me with the cup, which was a tankard. It is here in front of me as I write. It was the most perfect moment in my quest. So far.

3
New Clubs

I returned from Scotland more confident than ever – I had the Wedding Cup, after all – but there was a voice in the back of my head reminding me of sliced drives and missed putts. I decided that now was the time to get new clubs. I started wandering around golf shops picking up clubs and practising in front of the full-length mirrors. I had not quite taken up appearing in golf gear yet on the course, but golf is a kind of pantomime so maybe it wouldn't be long.

I took to disappearing down to American Golf in Watford and became a kind of golf fetishist, trying on golf gloves, fingering the balls, caressing the shafts of the drivers, balancing the putters in my hands, trying on the new waterproof golf trousers, and even assembling the new golf trolleys. There were rows and rows of irons, drivers and fairway woods. It seemed impossible to decide so I turned to Peter, the Harpenden professional, for advice.

Peter was delighted. He explained that I needed clubs that are made to measure and immediately I felt reassured.

He omitted to tell me of course they are much more expensive, but handmade is always better I told myself. We walked out to the area where he teaches and he brought some mats with him and an assortment of clubs. He measured me and decided my present clubs were too short. He was right. With longer clubs I could stand more upright without having to stoop to reach the ball. He passed me one of his clubs – a five iron – and asked me to do some practice swings. I brought the club sweepingly down but I misjudged the angle and the club thundered into the ground, there was a sickening sound and the club broke, the head separating from the shaft. I was acutely embarrassed but Peter was calm and assured me there was no problem.

We carried on with a number of other clubs and there were no more accidents. He measured me for a complete set of new irons. It was the least I could do for him after destroying one of his expensive clubs. I went home in a state of excitement. I didn't dare tell Heather the costs involved. She pressed me on this but I explained that Peter was giving me such a massive discount – a lie – that it was an irresistible bargain. It would be some weeks before my new clubs arrived.

'Well, you should use the time before they arrive to improve your own body, new clubs new body,' she said, and I knew she was right.

I was still a little overweight. Although I had already lost over a stone my body lacked flexibility. I couldn't touch my toes when I bent. Heather stood and effortlessly touched her toes, legs straight. I tried, but my arms dangled down just below my knees and no further.

'It's yoga for you,' she said.

I decided I needed another man to go with me, so I rang TW but he was surprisingly brisk. 'You must be joking,' he said. 'You won't get me there.'

'Come on, we can go to the pub afterwards and have a laugh.'

'No way.'

OK, so it would just have to be Heather and me and then Lesley decided to come as well and so a few days later we headed up to the St Albans Yoga Centre.

I was determined to try hard. I put on a new clean tee-shirt but there was a suspicious bulge just above my waist. It went when I drew my breath in but I decided that trying to keep my stomach in while I struggled to do the bends would be beyond me, so I settled on a loose-fitting blue Greg Norman golf shirt and dark blue tracksuit bottoms. I decided not to wear the white shorts I still have from school but I did slip on my school jockstrap which still has its name tape with my name and SCHOOL HOUSE embroidered on it in red. As I feared, I was the only man with fifteen women but the instructor, or yoga leader, or guru, was a man thank God.

I kept quiet. There were no candles, which was a relief, but there was some Indian music from a small music machine in the corner. We lay down on the mats and I decided I should keep away from Heather and Lesley, or rather they disappeared to the other end of the room – an old school hall. At least I was inside. At school I used to have to do PE outside every morning, jumping up and down to keep warm. Here it was warm and the soothing voice took me through the Sun Salutation.

This involved a sequence of lifting my arms above my head then dropping down into a forward bend, and then into a kind of press-up. Then we made a sort of cobra shape – this was clearly good for my back. Then I was required to jump my legs forward while crouching down. I pitched over to one side, and lay gasping. Everyone was so busy concentrating on their own movements that no one noticed me. I scrambled back but realised that Heather was now standing up and bending back, so I got to my feet and struggled to catch up. We went through the same sequence a few times but this was proving pretty tricky to keep up with. Suddenly I farted, caused no doubt by all the twisting and turning. No one said anything. I wondered if I should apologise but I stayed silent and after a bit I gave up and lay back on the mat and started to daydream.

I returned home in some pain, and my back felt more stiff and sore but Heather assured me this would pass and my shots would be like whiplash before long. I resolved to keep going.

It was July and the clubs were still not ready so I decided this was the time to head north for the Open at Royal Birkdale. I had always wondered what the professional player can teach the amateur. Perhaps I could learn something by watching them play.

I set off for Royal Birkdale early in the morning. I drove on motorways for a couple of hours until I turned off the M6 to follow the AA signs to the Open. It was only twenty miles but I was soon caught up in a jam as we struggled through Ormskirk, past delivery stations for a myriad of supermarkets, past road-improvement schemes and one-way diversions. I reached the countryside, and away I went down narrow lanes before more diversions took me through a large housing estate until I finally reached the Park and Ride in Southport. As I was being directed to my space I rolled down the window and explained to the policeman it had taken me an hour and a half to cover the twenty miles.

'Oh, yes, I am sorry,' the policeman explained, 'but during the night someone rearranged all the signs and the traffic is a shambles.'

Great.

Royal Birkdale lies just outside Southport, a few miles north of Liverpool. Wednesday was practice day. The bus dropped me near the entrance. I had already bought my ticket so I walked in. It smelt just like the circus, but no sign of any elephants or tigers, just tent after tent of official merchandise – Lexus cars, Pringle sweaters, and golf equipment. I resisted buying anything but I did sneak a look at the golf books, and wondered if I would ever master golf sufficiently to complete this book.

As ever it was very windy. I decided to walk the whole course and started at the first. Only people with passes can walk on the fairway so I made my way alongside the path. Everything was roped off. Three players were playing up the fairway – Lee Westwood, Ernie Els and Ian Poulter.

There was a large crowd at the first green with people shouting out good-naturedly to all the players. As they left the green they stood talking to everyone, and signing hats, programmes, whatever came to hand. I stood to one side. We went up to the second tee and I watched them driving into the wind. They were wonderfully composed and with perfect balance they drove the ball low over the rough down to the fairway. It was humbling to watch golf played with such ease. I reminded myself that these people practised every single day and I was simply a weekend golfer, a high handicapper.

I decided to wait on the second fairway for the next player. Then two balls came racing over the hill above landing just below me, and in a moment there was an American voice.

'I am really sorry about that,' said Tom Watson as he came into the rough. I could feel the flush of celebrity.

I showed him where his ball was which he picked up and threw back on to the fairway – it was practice day, after all – and fired a five iron 200 yards to the green. The course was perfect and I stood at the edge of the fairway marvelling at the quality of the ground, it was almost as good as the greens. I watched them on the edge of the green hitting the ball high into the air making the ball spin back when it hit the grass. Heather had always said she would never believe I was a proper golfer until I had learnt how to do that. When I had asked Peter about it he had simply laughed, which was bewildering, but I had never dared to tell Heather.

I then wandered across to the practice area by the fourteenth green. They were all there, everyone whom I had seen on television at tournaments all over the world – Miguel Angel Jimenez with his cigar, V. J. Singh, Sergio Garcia hitting straight shots for miles. The path up to the area was lined with kids and every player stopped and talked to them.

Greg Norman stopped for what seemed like hours signing and chatting. It was striking to see how much time they devoted to everyone.

I talked to the marshals who all came from the eighteen courses nearest to Birkdale; each club covered one hole, an old Open tradition. The seventeenth hole had been remodelled with curves and burrows all across the green and they all agreed that the changes weren't in keeping with the spirit of the course. For me it was simply impossible to judge where the ball would go and the shortest way to the hole, but the players seemed to have some uncanny feel for the lie of the land.

I walked across to the beer tent. It was full of men from Liverpool and I was struck by the laughter and banter. I wondered if there was anyone here from the golfing establishment, and then far away on the seventeenth fairway I spotted a man in red corduroy trousers.

It was late by now so I headed back to my base. Again I diligently followed the AA signs. It was a wild-goose chase but eventually I got to junction 27 and the Welcome Break hotel. The receptionist had no record of my booking, but gave me room nine over-looking the car park. I went in. Clearly a smoker had been there the night before. I tried to open the window and failed. There was no phone, no drinks cupboard, just one small towel and a soap dispenser. But at least there was a television. I sat on the bed and watched the news and the weather forecast which gave a severe weather warning for the next day. I searched the other channels, films and Sky Sports. All blocked.

I walked across to the receptionist to unblock the channels and asked her where the best place to eat was. She told me the choice was the Wimpy or the service station restaurant. It was raining by now. A night of Sky Sports and a Wimpy. And cars racing up and down the motorway. It all felt just too grim, so I picked up my bag, returned my key and headed for the car. A wimp of course, but after a day of witnessing such generosity and good humour I just couldn't face a night on my own. I felt lonely and decided it was madness to put up with all this, so got in the car and drove home. I remembered all the holidays with the children that we had left early. Every summer I took the kids away on my own, camping in Cornwall. It sounds so idyllic; the reality was trying to put up a tent on a cliff top with rain pouring down and serious wind, so serious that during the night the tent was ripped to pieces so we scrambled into the car, and, yes, drove home.

It may seem like quitting, but I had seen the course and the players and learnt that in the end they had nothing to tell me except that it was impossible for me ever to reach that level. I found the endless tents of merchandise depressing and realised that the target of all such salesmanship was the high handicapper. What all the tents whispered, or rather shouted, was that success was in the grasp of everybody, especially those with cash. I so much wanted to believe it was true but most golfers never even reach a hundred, let alone eighty. However, this irritation felt churlish and bad-tempered. It had been a joy to witness such perfectly controlled golf. I watched the tournament on television. It was extraordinarily windy and wet and then Greg Norman gave all us older players a fantastic boost. There was hope for us yet. Padraig Harrington won, beating Norman in the last round (they had gone out together) and even now I remember his glorious second shot on the seventeenth to the green.

Once back home I had a phone call from Peter saying my new clubs were ready. I was there before the day was out. They were pure, not a scratch, not a mark, no grass in the grooves. I decided I had to buy a new driver to match – there was a discount on a new Callaway, and by then it felt wrong not to buy a new bag as well. They all looked fantastic together and I lovingly placed the bag and clubs in the car. I decided I should head back to Aldeburgh.

4
Aldeburgh

I was back at Southwold ready to make an attack on Aldeburgh. I had not been on the course since the Packer competition in March. It was early August and I had over a whole year before the Packer was restaged in September. I had new clubs and had had lots of lessons, so this effort must have a pay-off. On Friday morning I got up early and drove south to Aldeburgh. I decided to buy a weekly ticket so I could play all week. Heather was coming up with TW and Lesley for the weekend, then the following week I would be on my own. The weather looked ominous as I teed up.

The wind was blowing straight down the first fairway so I was driving straight into it. The ball billowed and went right, barely reaching the fairway. I had a memory that this had happened before. Is this what they mean about your body having a memory, I wondered, and is it possible I will never hit a straight shot again on this hole? I hit a four iron into the wind, and the ball went into the bunker on the left, I struggled out and hit low over the green. I chipped back, three putts – a seven.

The second hole is largely downhill with treacherous bunkers halfway down the fairway so if the drive is off centre then almost certainly it is in one of the two bunkers, and yes it was. A six on a par four. The third is uphill into the wind, with a narrow fairway, all of 400 yards. I reached the green in three and then three putted, six again. There seemed little chance, in fact no chance of an eighty today. I was reminded of the pro telling me when I bought my ticket 'this is the hardest course in East Anglia'. It felt like the hardest course in the world.

The fourth is a short par three with bunkers surrounding the raised green and planking on the side of the bunkers. I drove into the bunker. I knew that if I mishit the bunker shot I was likely to get a ball in the face so I tamely hit out on to the grass. No heroics for me here.

The round continued much the same and I must in the end have scored over a hundred. I sat glumly in the clubhouse with a ham sandwich and a Rock Shandy.

I resolved to go out again for another eighteen holes. The first nine continued as before. I had to change my way of playing. It is funny that all the golf books say you have to concentrate on the positive and not worry about the bad shots, 'just move on' they say. Not for me, though God knows why I think I know better. I ditched my fancy new driver and went back to my original inexpensive driver and decided to play to my handicap, consciously using my extra shots.

On the tenth I drove straight down between the gorse bushes. I didn't go for the green but played a five iron short, but accurately, then chipped on to the green and finished four feet from the hole. My method seemed to be working but the putt was angled and sloping and the ball ran past. Oh well, a five. I played like that for the next four holes keeping it straight and sensible. I added my scores on the sixteenth.

At this point perhaps I should try to explain the golf system of pars and the Stableford system of scoring. Every hole has a par score, which is a score you should get if you were a good golfer – for a par four, a drive, a shot from the fairway on to the green, two putts. There are usually eighteen holes on a golf course. Most of these will be par fours. If the hole is longer than usual then the par is five, you are allowed an extra shot to get on to the green; if it is shorter then the par is three, so your drive should reach the green.

Most players have a handicap – if it is one, you are really good, if twenty-eight then you are not. To get a handicap you have to fill up three cards over three rounds and give them to the golf club. They average your score then calculate how many shots you are over the total par score. So the par might be seventy-two shots and if you score ninety then your handicap would be eighteen – the difference between the two. The handicap system allows people of differing abilities to compete against one another. So if a player with a handicap of ten plays the twenty handicapper, the latter has an extra ten shots allocated over a number of holes. Each of the eighteen holes is arranged in order of difficulty so the extra shots are placed against the trickiest holes.

OK, so each player has a handicap and each hole has a par. The Stableford system is a system of allocating points to every hole. Let me give an example. I have a handicap of seventeen which allows me a shot on every hole except one.

The first hole is a par four. I play it and take five shots. My handicap allows me one shot, so I take that one shot from the five, hence four shots. The Stableford system allocates points, so if you have a four you get two points. If I had scored a three then I get three points, a bogey (one over) then one point. This is after my handicap has been taken off my actual score. So for a round if I played to my handicap I would score thirty-six points. If I do better then it is over thirty-six, worse lower than thirty-six. I need to do better if I am to have any chance of winning the Packer.

Back now to the real golf. I turned to the seventeenth, a par three, quite simple, but I sliced the ball and it bounced off the green at the back. I mishit an eight iron back, leaving it short. The hole is tucked away among the folds in a small hollow but I had to run the putt over a small mound. I failed, again leaving it short, so it needed two more putts. Five shots, no points. On to the eighteenth. A straight drive – the hole is over 450 yards, then a sensible seven iron up to a treacherous bunker lying halfway across the fairway, and then I took a five wood to hit it to the green. It was almost my last shot, but the ball skidded to the right and into another looming bunker. I came out sideways, overhit the green with a wedge, struggled back, two putts – a seven.

I rang Heather from the car.

'I did really well,' I babble, 'but messed up on the eighteenth.'

There is silence, then she says, 'But don't you always mess up on some hole or other?'

Yes, of course, she is right – something always goes wrong. However, I am not dismayed. The next day she came up with TW and Lesley. I arranged to meet them at Aldeburgh. We had lunch in the clubhouse. I couldn't believe it but Heather loved it. It is old and comfortable and the people there were charming. We gazed out over the first fairway as we ate our sandwiches.

Aldeburgh feels easy and companionable. Lesley and Heather drove home. TW and I played golf. Fun, but poor scores. A ninety-two.

The three left on Sunday morning so I headed back to Aldeburgh. All those golf adverts say you are in a competition between yourself and the course. I was fed up with delving into my 'golf mind', twisting and turning in a morass of panic and guilt. So I decided to concentrate on the vagaries of the golf *course*. If I could get that right then my mind would follow and the golf would improve. In theory.

So that morning I simply played to my handicap and respected the course. Went with the flow, as they say. I kept to the plan through the first nine, scoring nineteen points, the bonus being I parred the eighth which was a three. The back nine was not so good, though I scored on each hole but had a run from the eleventh to the fourteenth of double bogeys (two over par) which finished with a score of thirty-one. I think much of this was due to the rain which started to pour down on the tenth and I had no towel so just got soaked.

Sunday afternoon was to be a better round. No more

rain but very strong breezes coming off the sea which meant a fair mixture of cross and facing winds. I started so well, holing a long putt across the green for a four at the first. All this rather went to my head, then I sliced the ball towards the second, taking a six. The third was worse, and I hooked my second – a six iron – into the gorse and it looked as if the round was all over. But there are miracles. On the short fourth usually I am in the bunkers or the gorse, but not this time. I hit my pitch to the back of the green, with a long sloping putt needed to get back to the hole. I stroked it perfectly and moved from the left and into the hole. What bliss, a birdie.

I bogeyed the next few holes with one aberration on the sixth and reached the ninth, a long drive from high up towards the clubhouse. It was straight, as was the five iron leaving me sixty yards short. I decided to run up a five iron under the wind – it worked, leaving me a ten-foot putt which, curving from the right, went in. Nine holes done with eighteen points and playing to my handicap, which was good.

The next three holes went perfectly. Straight drives, five irons short then running the ball into the heart of the green scoring three pars on the trot.

Then I met someone I knew, chatted, decided to let the people behind through, and added up my score. What a mistake. It looked really good, but the gods were out to get me for my hubris. I returned to the fourteenth, slicing the ball from one side to another, scoring a six. The next hole is a short three, which I had parred before. Today was no such day. I mishit the drive into the bracken, lost. I played another but finished with a score of seven.

It was all slipping away from me. The wind was whipping across the fairways as I turned to the long sixteenth, which is a four. I decided I had to play it safe and calmly which I did, straight down the fairway, a couple of putts. A six, which was fine. The seventeenth is a par three, no stroke here, but I hit it on to the green, two putted for a three, and turned for home.

The first two shots were fine, leaving me one hundred yards into the green. It looked so easy and I decided to come into the green from the right. I made it too difficult by aiming right, sliced it and it raced away into the bunker. I hacked at it in the gorse, it skidded a few feet nearer the hole and I finished with a seven. As Heather says, it always goes wrong somewhere. Yes, but adding it all up I scored thirty-five points – not enough to win yet respectable.

What lessons, I asked myself sitting in the car? Don't stop. Don't add up the scores. Don't think any shot is easy, there are gremlins hiding everywhere. Distrust all advice.

The course is a wonder but even more wonderful is the club. Everyone talks to everyone else. Even I talked to some I didn't know. I had more golf conversations here in three days than I had in Harpenden in a year. Everyone is easy and yes there is a dress code but no one shouts at you from across the fairway to tuck your shirt in, as had happened to me a week before at Harpenden. You have to wear a jacket in the smoking room, an odd dark room at the end of a passage which I have been too nervous to enter, and long socks when out on the course, but this seems a small price for the conviviality. Single players are respected. No one is allowed to go off the tenth if there is anybody on the ninth, so different from my usual course which uses the thirteenth as if it was the first hole, with no respect, of course, for the single player – 'go back to the first' someone told me as they waited for the fourth player to join them. Somehow I felt this could never happen here. One other thing: virtually everybody carries their clubs, men and women, so the game whirrs along. No four-balls, only two-ball foursomes, so the game is quick. Good, plain, well-mannered golf. I was utterly charmed, and it reminded me just how marvellous the game can be. I felt I should abandon all those parkland courses; this seemed like the real thing. I drove back to Southwold, pulled on my trunks and ran into the rough sea. There were only one or two people in the water and I imagined they were of course fellow golfers from Aldeburgh. Real men. Like me. But I didn't talk to them, that would be a step too far.

I felt I was perhaps playing too much golf so Heather decided to drive over later that day. It's not far from St Albans, after all. Until she arrived I settled down to work. Work for me means reading, planning and phoning.

For many years I was a publisher. I had started as a copy-editor at Routledge and Kegan Paul in Carter Lane, just below St Paul's. I still have the letter offering me the job. After surviving two years learning the intricacies of copy-editing I slowly began to commission academic books. Routledge also had a tiny fiction list and I was allowed to publish a novel by Christopher Hope called *A Separate Development*. Set in South Africa, it was a brilliant account of life under apartheid. It won the David Higham Prize for the best first novel. At the prize-giving Christopher thanked me and mentioned, casually, how especially grateful he was to me as every other publisher in London had rejected the manuscript. I was shocked as I had thought I was the first person to have seen the book, typical publishing hubris, but actually it was the best lesson I could ever have learnt, simply to trust my own judgement.

I then went to Heinemann, mainly to jazz up the list. It was extremely grand – I had never been in a lift in a publishing house before. The company was hugely successful, every year there was a new book by Wilbur Smith and Catherine Cookson which sold in huge numbers. My books generally were good but rarely sold in any numbers. They needed me to bring in some prize-winning authors. So I went out diligently to woo as many good writers as I could. My first lucky break was Graham Swift. He had finished his third novel and his old publisher wasn't convinced by it. This was *Waterland* and only missed winning the Booker by a whisker.

I switched across then to Seckers only for a very short time but time enough to have too many fights. My time was up, so I took a job with Granta. Bill Buford, the editor, had come to Southwold with the owner Rea Hederman to seek me out one summer. They were walking around the town wearing dark suits and dark glasses asking for me, and we eventually met in a pub. I took the job – to set up a literary department – and duly arrived one Monday morning to start work. I was shown to a desk in a large room and waited for Bill to arrive. When he did he went straight into his room and shut the door. I remember it so clearly even now. Pompously I felt I had given up a lot and didn't fancy hanging around to fit in with Bill's moods. I drove home that night and decided it wasn't for me and so an elaborate dance began to get me to Cape, then being run by Tom Maschler – I never returned to Granta, didn't speak to Bill for at least two years and was never paid. It was the right decision, it was Bill's show after all and he didn't need me. Probably one of the few geniuses I have come across in publishing. A total maverick, exasperating but a truly exceptional talent.

Cape is a literary publishing house and had recently been taken over by the American corporation Random House. I was the new broom but it was Maschler's show. He had sold it to the Americans and he was involved with all the authors, lines of stars. I was certainly the interloper. I had my successes, notably Ben Okri who won the Booker Prize with *The Famished Road*. Even then Maschler was the first out of the chair to embrace Ben. It was a hard battle to win, but over five years I put up a real fight and then it was time to review how the company was run. I had been running it rather one-sidedly and looking back now probably somewhat irresponsibly, just a bit anyway. I had a reputation for being headstrong, difficult and extravagant. I did not fit into the new corporate regime, there had been a lot of changes to the board and my face just didn't fit any more. There was no other publishing company I could work for or wanted to work for – Cape was the best – and I had always fought for the writers, possibly too much, so I decided to be a literary agent. I knew a bit about it having spent most of my working life buying books from them.

Virtually all writers have agents, though there are exceptions. I joined an established agency run by Gillon Aitken who agreed to pay me for a year to see how it went. There was no space in his office so as a temporary measure we rented a room in the old Penguin building off the King's Road. It had just been vacated when Penguin moved to the old Shell building in the Strand. I was the only person in this block of six storeys; my office was actually a whole floor, probably the largest ever inhabited by a publisher or agent. First I hoped many of the people I had published would come to me. Ted Walker, a poet, came at the beginning of that first week. He came to see me and was obviously so appalled at my new office that by the end of the week he had returned to his previous agent. So at the end of the first week I still had no clients. Things did look up and I gradually accumulated a list of clients but several of them already had contracts in place which they had to fulfil, so the money continued to go to their old agents who had done the original negotiations, as is the convention.

I had started in September but by the following spring it was clear that I was being paid more than I was earning – it is very easy to calculate an agent's earnings. It's a regular percentage of the advances that are negotiated. Gillon called me over and explained that he felt this arrangement was not working out but he urged me to start up on my own and he very nobly suggested that he guarantee an overdraft so I could start an agency with at least some backing. I drove home wondering how on earth I could explain all this to Heather.

She was having lunch as I came into the house.

'What are you doing here?' she asked.

'I think now might be the right time to start a new literary agency,' I blurted out.

'You're mad,' she said.

I had then to explain exactly what had happened and that really we had very little choice.

However, we did agree on one important thing: that we were not going to take any of Gillon's money, generous though he had been. We would succeed or fail by ourselves. So we divided up the tasks: Heather would do the money, I would do the deals. We were terrified; Heather knew nothing about invoices, or VAT and contracts. I had a handful of clients but as I had done all those deals for them when I was with Gillon, he wanted all the income, and he was entitled to it. So with no income, four children, a large mortgage but lots of optimism we set to work. Not that different really from trying to break eighty.

Anyway, this is not a history of what eventually became David Godwin Associates Ltd, but it explains roughly what I do when I am not striding up and down fairways.

Heather arrived but I decided after all that I must keep going with my golf.

Round five. A blowy day but no rain. I set off determined not to stop or count my score and I kept to that plan. The first two holes went well but the third was becoming my disaster hole. Last time I lost two balls – the hole is a par four, 416 yards, but in the Packer rules this becomes a par five (Simon loves to meddle with the scores and make some holes easier, thank God). The tee is set low down and you have to drive slightly right to avoid a bunker 230 yards up on the left. There is thick grass all up the left and gorse on the right as the fairway rises from the tee. The wind was running from the left. My drive wobbled on to the fairway – poorly hit but straight at least. I took a five iron to move it forward so I could come into the green which doglegs to the left. The five was short, missing the next bunker. Just a half-hit eight now to the green underneath the wind. I mishit it and it went to the left under the gorse. I searched for it but it had gone, hiding no doubt in some rabbit hole, again. I dropped another and hoofed it over the green at the back, another eight iron, short, much too short and then two putts. An eight. I felt like going home. But golf is an optimistic game, so I went on to the fourth and kept going. I finished the nine with four pars and on I went to the back nine.

The sun was shining, and I kept my head with only one aberration on the short fifteenth – the five iron stumbled off the tee into the rough, I then whacked it too hard and the ball raced over the green, three back for a five, but with a stroke I had at least one point. I finished with a six on the long par four, the eighteenth.

I sat in the car and counted my score. Forty-three shots on the front nine, forty-four on the back nine – eighty-seven.

I felt joyous, thirty-six points and I had only messed up two holes, and missed four short putts so eighty was doable. At last I felt I could succeed, and the few days playing every day seemed to be working. I felt much more confident except for the third hole with its alarming twists and turns and usually played against the wind. I drove home making a new plan for the third. That would do it.

I had three more days to go lower. Unfortunately my game did not improve.

On Wednesday morning I met someone I recognised from Southwold Golf Club who was trying to find out how to become a member of Aldeburgh. We chatted in the car park, and then I asked him if he fancied a game. I thought perhaps it would be good for me to play with someone for a change. He challenged me to matchplay – you win or lose every hole whatever your cumulative score – so I should put away my card. I was very confident; all this practice would now pay off.

He had never been on the course before so as we played I talked him through the difficult holes, the bunker placings, the tricky greens and I suddenly realised I was three holes down. Hubris again. I thought I would get some holes back though – I bogeyed the seventh, hit a nice floating six to the eighth green, his was perched on the far edge of the green after a lucky bounce. He putted first, a long putt of maybe thirty-five feet. The ball came straight up the green; I lifted the flag and in it dropped. I could not believe it – 'great putt' I called, my gut wrenched as I tried to match it, but failed. Back to four down, and down was the right word.

However, I struggled to make back some holes as he ballooned his drives into the gorse. Two holes conceded so I was two down with four to go. Surely pure determination would drive me back. I won the sixteenth, one down. We faced a 200-yard par three with the wind behind. I took a five iron and hit it short into the rough. He hit his four to the left of the green, chipped across and putted in for a three. Two down with one to play. I had lost. It was a real job to mask my desperation but I shook him by the hand, it is only a game after all, but I wanted to hide in the bushes. Such vanity. We played the last hole. I got into the car and drove home.

I raced into the sea, it was glorious, the beach was almost empty, and the sun came out and suddenly that golf game did not seem to matter any more. However, I still faced the dilemma of how to play with someone *and* keep my concentration.

My final game was on Thursday, it was windy and it was not a good day. Perhaps I had played too much, maybe I had taken on too much, and maybe the goal was impossible. I felt defeated. I read through all my cards. I felt really fed up with myself and I thought back to the Eden course when I had scored thirty-nine on the back nine to win my only championship cup. Then I saw those other depressing scores. Cards littered with sevens and eights. Maybe it was the wind, yes it was the wind and too much fussing about my putts, which so often have wobbled their way towards the hole then veered off to the left or right, and found some extra slope to run down, a slope invisible to the naked eye. I decided I must simply focus on the hole and not worry any more about my feet or where my eye is. The hole is the thing. Putt it.

It had been a long week, and I had hardly spoken to anyone. But there had been some sublime moments: when I hit a five iron on the seventh to within three feet of the pin – and away from the golf course when two goldfinches came to a feeding basket in the garden, so luminous. Now I was off home. The golf clubs were back in the shed; no more golf, for a bit at least. There was always hope and Harpenden was much easier, flat greens and no wind. Heaven.

5

Cornwall

Towards the end of the season I decided to treat myself to a visit to Cornwall, and after that, I would face one final challenge. I put my name down for the November Stableford competition in Harpenden. Halfway down the sheet pinned up in the bar someone's name had been deleted which left a spare place; I scribbled down my name and was set to play with Mr Lewis and Mr Wilson. I then headed for Cornwall where I had arranged to meet my sister Mary.

I had lived in Cornwall as a child. My father was in the RAF and was stationed there when we returned from Kuala Lumpur in Malaya where he had been posted during the 'troubles', as they were always called. We lived in married quarters at St Eval airfield. It is on the north coast a few miles inland from Padstow. I remember very little about it, except picking mushrooms with my father in the early morning. I went back a few years ago and stood outside the house we lived in and was unable to recall one single detail of the interior. My primary school was around the corner. I presume there were heaps of

RAF kids there, but strangely nothing of that time survives in my memory. I *do* know that I stayed there until I reached the ripe old age of seven when I was sent away to prep school at Ashdown House in Kent. It was a terrible time; the dormitories were full of seven- and eight-year-olds crying themselves to sleep. I was one of them. I had elocution lessons to rid me of my Cornish accent. It was the Greek play that did it – I was the messenger to Agamemnon and my accent overwhelmed the ancient Greek. But Cornwall never left me.

When my father left the RAF we moved away from Cornwall but always went back for our summer holidays. We often stayed at the golf club at Trevose just outside Padstow and a few miles from St Eval. Occasionally I played with my father. He was a large man and a clumsy and erratic golfer so I played rarely. He was happier in the bar than on the fairway. He bought drinks for everyone and seemed to know everybody. I was bewildered, unable to handle all the jollity and embarrassed by my father's largesse. I remember asking him about the soda syphon on the bar so he showed me how it worked by squirting it all over me. Everyone laughed but I never asked him again how something worked. Maybe here was the start of my social unease, my wariness of clubs and bars.

But I love Cornwall. The beaches. So often I'm told how extraordinary the beaches are in South Africa and Australia but for me they are no match for Cornwall. In the early sixties I was one of the first to have a surf- board there. Made of solid wood, it was so big and heavy that I could barely drag it into the water. When I did

I took off my glasses and was effectively a blind surfer with a board like a tree. God knows how I never hit anyone. But this surfer is now a golfer. Two of my sons surf and I sometimes stand on the green of the fourth hole at Trevose scanning the sea to spot them amongst the waves.

My sister, Mary, has a house at Treyarnon Bay just along the coast. We met to play golf. Trevose has a clubhouse which has views over the whole course and out to sea. It has huge windows. The first tee is high and the fairway heads straight out towards the sea, the second reaches the dunes then the course runs along the beach then turns to the right and inland. The fourth is an exquisite hole with a dogleg to the left. It is a par five and the green almost reaches down to the rocks above Boobies Bay. The waves roll in great blocks, the wind flicking the surf off the crests.

Mary is a good golfer and we played well. We were the last couple out so we returned to the clubhouse in the setting sun with shadows across the fairways. I did not bother with keeping any scores. We ate in the golf club and I didn't feel haunted by any ghosts. It was good to be back. We returned to Padstow for a drink where my dad used to drink and we would then wait patiently outside. I was allowed inside this time and I also showed Mary the crazy golf course alongside the harbour wall. I had played there once with my sons Sebastian and Hugo who decided to play a kind of wild game chipping balls from one hole to another randomly. The only other time I had played crazy golf was with Heather. We were in Lowestoft – that morning I had been in the garage getting my bike fixed and the man there thought Southwold was so dull that he couldn't understand why anyone went. 'Get to Lowestoft,' he said, 'there's more fun there,' so when I told this to Heather we were in the car in seconds heading up the A12. We played on the pier then headed for the crazy golf course. How anyone imagined this game I can hardly believe, but we putted on concrete, through castles, round bends and corners, and the final hole had a drop of several feet. Heather won.

Back in Padstow the crazy course was shut.

The next day I drove home and on the Friday went to Harpenden to gear myself up for the competition. The temporary greens were being used because the greens themselves were soaked through. I played a few holes and somehow the fact that the temporary greens were almost part of the fairway took me back to the original golf holes in Scotland where they are literally at the end of the fairway. I would play in the competition the next day even if they were still using the temporary greens although I had been warned that over half the competitors would drop out in protest.

The following morning I hoped to find the car park overflowing and a real sense of occasion: Harpenden's answer to the Open. No such thing. The car park was almost empty, a few people shouted to each other. I arrived at the thirteenth to be met by Bob the marshal and soon after Mr Wilson and Mr Lewis arrived. We shook hands.

'I'm John.'

'I'm Malcolm.'

John and Malcolm were friends of one another, not me. I drove first, feeling very nervous. The drive went straight and I was off. John played off nineteen, Malcolm fourteen. Malcolm lost three balls in the first two holes, and John played bewilderingly fast. He had a low swing moving the club very fast down from a short backswing. The ball veered everywhere. On the fairway he simply raced to the ball, hit it quickly and it usually corkscrewed away to his right. He told me he had once done a round scoring only two points even with a handicap of nineteen. I could believe it. He was obsessed with going at full speed so there was no time to linger on the putts, no time to weigh up the line and I wondered how I could be so intimidated.

From green to green I three-putted while John and Malcolm had a great time, careering from hole to hole chatting and laughing, greeting other competitors on nearby greens and I began to realise that for them it was a terrific social occasion. They were really enjoying themselves. Yes the golf mattered, but not really. I again felt a bit of a fanatic, but I simply couldn't play golf like this. I slipped away and made myself a bacon sandwich at home. I began to worry whether this was all a terrible mistake. Maybe golf was for sociable geriatrics with power trolleys. My wife needed to wear bulky pale cardigans and to look after the flowers. Maybe too I envied them and was in some way jealous of their easy familiarity. Yes, that was probably nearer the truth. Golf can accommodate all sorts and perhaps I had to learn to do the same.

I found myself brooding on what I had learnt since

the Packer Tournament in the spring. I had new clubs and had played a lot but I was not sure I was getting better. I had been to the Open and watched innumerable golf matches on television. It got so bad that as soon as Heather went out for the evening I would switch to the Golf channel and be poised to switch over as soon as I heard her key in the door. Golf porn, no less.

I wondered if I really had it in me to make the grade, but I was optimistic. Another day. Now the winter was coming in, my stack of golf books were ready and I disappeared to sit and read them in front of the fire. I even had James Braid's book on advanced techniques in golf, published in 1911. Certain to sort me out.

6

India

In January I was off to India to the Jaipur Literary Festival. It occurred to me that this might be a golden opportunity to explore some new golf courses, keep my hand in and possibly pick up some new tips. I did not mention this plan to Heather as she was beginning to worry that I was becoming a serious addict.

India had always brought me luck so maybe it would again. I flew to Delhi, left my luggage in the hotel and headed for the Delhi Golf Club. I already knew my way around Delhi – my first visit there had been some years earlier, a time before golf.

After I had been dispatched from Gillon's office, I rented a desk amongst some shipping brokers in Covent Garden. It was on the first floor and had some rather palatial stairs up from the reception desk. Visitors were kept downstairs so I that I could sweep down giving the impression that there was further grandeur upstairs, rather than my solitary desk in a corner with a phone and little else. No filing cabinets, no fax machine, no executive clobber. One of my early clients was Patrick French who had written a biography of Sir Francis Younghusband, who had been part of the attempted English takeover of Southern Asia. One evening we walked over to the Nehru Centre in Mayfair for a talk he was about to give. He told me he had heard of a novel that a friend of his had just agreed to publish. The novelist was Arundhati Roy, the publisher Pankaj Mishra at HarperCollins in India and the novel as yet had no title. 'Of course, I would love to see it,' I said, so Patrick agreed to find some way to get me the manuscript. We had no emails then.

A week later a parcel arrived – very tightly packed and sealed, as all Indian parcels seem to be. I took it home and started to read: 'May in Ayemenem is a hot, brooding month. The days are long and humid. The river shrinks and black crows gorge on bright mangoes in still, dustgreen trees.'

I read on and here was a miraculous new voice. The story seemed to start at the end but it was told with such extraordinary skill, it was irresistible. I managed to get Pankaj's number but the person I wanted to speak to was Arundhati herself. Pankaj gave me her number and also said he had sent the novel to HarperCollins in London.

By this time I was so swept up in the book I could barely read it. I rang Arundhati and told her how fantastic I thought it was but she felt I was being a little premature to ring her when I hadn't actually finished it. She told me to finish it then call her. I spent the next day reading it to the end, then I called her and said I wanted to come and see her in Delhi. I had never been to India and had no interest in Indian literature but this was obviously a brilliant book and I was desperate to represent it. It was also perfectly clear to me that if she came to London to find an agent I was going to find it hard to make any impression when there were lots of other established agents around. She was puzzled and a little bewildered but we agreed to meet.

I needed a visa and after a quick trip to India House that was sorted, I bought a ticket and off I went. As Heather was driving me to Heathrow she asked me what inoculations I had had and whether I'd bought any malaria pills. The simple answer was no – it had never occurred to me, after all I was only going for two days. I had no pills, just blind faith that everything would be OK.

I arrived in Delhi and had no idea what to expect but the first thing I noticed as I came down to the immigration desks was a phone on the wall which was for free calls into the city. I had booked a hotel near where Arundhati lived and she had suggested that we should meet at the hotel. I used the phone to ring her and she said she would come over and meet me in the lobby. I described myself and then got a taxi through the swirling traffic to the hotel.

Arundhati soon appeared. She was small and very striking. I was big and clumsy. I managed to get into her small car, just. Her flat was at the top of a house and to reach it we had to crawl through a small trapdoor at the top of the stairs. There were a lot of dogs.

We began to talk about the book and I explained why I thought she might need me and how the publishing industry worked. I had also brought with me a copy of Michael Ondaatjee's poems and she seemed pleased. I had tea sitting on the ground with my legs sticking out beside me.

The phone kept ringing. Then I heard her say, 'I think you should speak to my agent.'

I was thrilled that she had chosen me. She passed me the phone and it was Stuart Proffitt from HarperCollins in London.

'What the hell are you doing there?' he asked.

'I came to see Arundhati and now I'm her agent,' I explained.

He was stunned that I had got there before him. It all ended happily. He bought the book and when it was published it went on to win the Booker Prize and sold all over the world. Would some of that luck rub off on my golf?

Delhi Golf Club is in the centre of the city, a huge green space but wherever you are on the course you can hear the traffic and the hooting of the taxis. The course was built by the Brits in 1931 and there are actually two: the Lodhi course and the Peacock course. The land was originally the burial ground of the fourteenth-century Lodhi dynasty so all over the course there are Muslim temples and shrines. The cabbie dropped me in the car park just after six in the morning to avoid the heat and I went through to see the starter. I had already been there the day before to check out the procedures, and a friend who was a member had arranged for me to borrow some clubs from one of her family who was a member but virtually never played. I explained all this to a starter who shouted to one of the many men in green tops. He was sent over to the store to get the clubs. I was then allocated a ball spotter and the three of us were then sent across to the sixth tee. I joined three other men, who it turned out were all working for the government.

The government owned the course and those who worked for the government could play whenever they wished alongside the real members. There was a sign beside the tee saying MONSOON RULES. These were the equivalent, they explained to me, of our winter rules. We teed up and all four of us, one after another, sliced our drives into the trees. Our ball spotters went into the trees and when we reached them our balls had been laid out in a neat row on the edge of the fairway. We played for three holes which brought us back to the side of the clubhouse. My partners brushed off the grass from their shoes. I watched, then followed them into the clubhouse. Tea, they explained. Glasses of marsala tea were brought to us along with a plate of buttered toast with ginger to one side which we placed on the toast. Delicious.

We were then called – it was time to return to the golf – and when we reached the first we were told to go to the tenth. We went past a sign saying NO STOPPING AFTER THE FIFTH. There was a group of fourteen men waiting on the tee. I looked down the fairway and could count a further thirty-two people in front of us. My partners decided it was too long to wait – they had to go to work, it was now just after eight and getting hotter. There was a lot of bustle and the starter there assured me that I could play on my own behind the party now on the tee. I am used to old golfers but this sight reached a new level. None of them were fit enough to put their own tees in the ground, the caddies did that and their drives barely scrambled on to the fairway. They moved slowly and sedately forward. Two of them were wearing what looked like girdles laced at the back. I waited to play but it was a long wait. I could at least admire the birds and peacocks. On the scorecard every hole has a bird attached to it so I spent my time scanning the fairways while waiting to play – the orange-breasted green pigeon (the sixteenth), the red-vented Bubul (the third) and the streaked fantail warbler on the tenth. There was no question of being let through. As the starter had explained he had already sent through twenty-three groups of four men since 5.30 that morning.

Eventually another three golfers caught up with me and we played the last two holes as a four. It had taken four hours to play nine holes. God, I thought Harpenden was slow. It was now too hot so I paid off my team – how much, I asked them, but they refused to name a figure. I gave them each 200 rupees but it was clear it wasn't enough so I added a further hundred. I then decided I should play on a more modern course I had heard of outside Delhi at Gurgaon. It promised to be another early start.

I was staying with a friend on the fourteenth floor of a huge block of flats in Gurgaon. This is the New India, blocks of flats barely four years old overlooking a mass of houses below.

I waited outside with my bag and golf shoes. I was being taken by Mr Ravi Purri to the golf course he managed roughly twenty-five miles away. I climbed into the car and as we avoided a group of wild pigs on the road he told me the history of the course. It was the first private course to be built in India. Three hundred acres of agricultural land had been bought and after a lot of wrangling it has been designated as a suitable location. Jack Nicklaus was engaged to design it. It is hard to imagine the sight of the great golfer wandering over such raw land. Ravi and I talked about the challenges facing India. He explained the major problem was one of infrastructure. You only had to look at the road to understand this. Hundreds of cyclists, buses, trucks, rickshaws and cars struggled along, with cars going in different directions, tractors crossing the traffic and large amounts of water on the road. We turned off the highway and headed towards the course. It was five and a half miles and it took us nearly an hour to reach it the road was so bad. This was the road to one of the finest golf courses in India, a road so potholed that at times we simply bounced along. I held on to the handle above the door the whole time. Ravi explained that the road would have to be improved for the course to succeed.

We arrived. I was given a set of clubs and a classic golf-club shirt. We set off, me and Ravi sharing a buggy, the only red golf cart. It was seven in the morning, the course was empty. I cannot imagine a more wonderful place to play golf. The first hole lay before us, idyllic. Birds, trees, a breeze, the fairways perfect, the greens too, especially after the horror of the slow greens in Delhi. Ravi explained there were over 140 people employed to maintain it. At one point I counted six people sitting in one bunker pulling up stray weeds, all wearing what looked like miners' helmets. Ravi had told

me that this was a favourite course for Koreans, especially
Korean women. There was famously a group of twenty-
four who played every day completely covered from the
sun so their perfectly white complexions would never
be compromised.

After ten holes we had breakfast: scrambled eggs, tea
and toast. Ravi left. The colonel had arrived. He had
recently retired from the Indian cavalry. He looked the
part, a wide-brimmed hat, a white long-sleeved tee-shirt
underneath a brown top, mirrored sunglasses. Over breakfast he told me how to ride a polo pony, how the bit
on the pony's mouth worked, how their heads should
never be allowed to drop. He told me I should drink
coconut milk — the best cure yet for hangovers.

He strode on to the tenth tee and lashed the ball way
to the left. The fairways were wide but not wide enough
for the colonel. He marched up the fairway mostly
disdaining the golf cart. He continued his drive routine
on the next hole despite his phone ringing incessantly.
I played erratically but it didn't matter. Standing on the
sixteenth I trusted my caddy as he passed me a six iron.
And it landed on the green inches from the hole. I putted
it for a birdie and went to the seventeenth feeling very
chuffed. I mishit the ball into the bushes inches off the
tee, so the ball spotter went into the bushes as I drove
another ball and swept up the fairway in my buggy. After
the eighteenth we went off for lunch — a simple vegetarian
meal: vegetable biryani, daal, chapattis, traditional food
in the most modern of settings.

Then I was whisked home through the traffic. Back
to the towers of Gurgaon.

I wanted to make sense of this so I went to see Namita Gokhale and we set off with a friend into the streets of Old Delhi to have some street food. We drove past the golf club and she explained how important the golf club was to the social life of Delhi. She had inherited her membership from her father, though she had never played golf, but she always voted in the elections for the new chairman. It was a Raj golf course and anyone who played golf wanted to play there. It wasn't the best golf course – far from it – but it meant something. We got out of the car and got on to a rickshaw. We struggled through the tiny streets with wires and cables criss-crossing the sky, strung between buildings. We ate kebabs cooked in front of us, a potato dish called aloo tikki, basically potato cakes with curd and tamarind, finishing with semolina. The food was fabulous and everyone ate with their fingers, amidst the noise and bustle of the street. India is overcrowded, golf courses included. Delhi golf is woven into the city and I realised that the Gurgaon course was almost too perfect a golf oasis in India. By being outside the city it remained disconnected from the city. Ravi had driven me round a building plot on the edges of the fairway and very soon too the houses would be up and Delhi would be arriving on the new golf course. I had caught it at a moment of virginity, so it was an experience of pure golf. Yes, golf did tell me something about India but I carried no real tips to help me with my game except to wish I had a ball spotter and a caddie to go round Aldeburgh with me. Fat chance.

Jaipur Literary Festival is held every year in the third week of January. It has grown from a small event involving a dozen writers, one venue and maybe 250 people to six venues, over 200 writers and an audience in excess of 40,000. All the events are free, and every night there is music from all over India and Pakistan. I had spotted a golf course outside the town. I went out late one afternoon but it was a dismal course – I felt spoilt after the two Delhi courses – so I went back to the festival: thousands of people to hear Vikram Seth, but no golf talk.

7

The Old Tonbridgians

After a long winter the end of March finally arrived and with it the beginning of the new golf season. I was off to Aldeburgh to take part in the first competition of the new year. My back was stiff, but I had new balls, the clubs were all cleaned and I was ready to go. It is the Old Tonbridgian Spring Golf Match and I wonder how on earth this has come about.

I had had virtually no dealings with my old school for over forty years yet here I was about to set off to play in an Old Boys' tournament. Is this a tribute to golf, I wondered, that it could make me do the most surprising things? Perhaps it was the lure of Aldeburgh itself that tugged me back but I had not forgotten my previous disasters: eight on the sixteenth, lost in the bunker on the third. But I told myself to be confident. And now I had to meet my fellow members of School House.

I wondered if I would recognise anybody except my golfing partner Gerald. It was Gerald who was responsible really for this. It was he who dragged me back over ten years previously to an Old Boys' dinner. There I met the boy who had dominated my school years. We met when I was seven. I idolised him. He was charming, charismatic and rebellious. He went on to Oxford after Tonbridge and I barely saw him again until the reunion. He had just had a bad car accident and had a large scar across his cheek. He was drinking. He was obsessed with trying to get his sons into Tonbridge and spent his time buttonholing teachers and even the headmaster. I was embarrassed and slipped away. I never had any plans for my own sons to go to Tonbridge or indeed any boarding school. Soon I found myself talking to Andrew Dunlop, a person I had had little time for at school, yet now he was the most interesting person there. So much for child-hood friends.

I had only recently joined the Old Tonbridgians so that I could play in this tournament. I slipped into the car park. It was full of men. I recognised no one; mind you it was over forty years since I had seen most of them. I introduced myself to the secretary, practised some shots then headed for the tenth tee. I was paired with David Summers.

'How nice to meet you,' I said shaking his hand, 'which house were you in?'

'School House, where you were,' he replied, 'don't you recognise me?'

'Of course, of course,' I said.

I had no idea who he was.

We teed off and made our way down the fairway. All the talk was of how our lives had changed. My golf was awful; somehow it seemed impossible for me to combine golf and chat. We talked of the evening to come, which came soon enough. Black tie, minutes of the AGM to be agreed, then into supper. All white men.

We sat down in the Aldeburgh Golf Club dining room.

'What do you do?' I asked the man opposite.

'I travel,' he replied, as if travelling was a kind of job but I soon realised that almost everyone was retired. The subject of India came up. I told them my India story and about some of the writers I represented but no one had heard of any of them which put me firmly in my place. A man sitting nearby knew about India though.

'Do you know Twinkly Bottom?' he enquired.

'Not sure that I do.'

'Well you should go there when you are in Calcutta, along with the Fairlawn Hotel. It's run by Mrs Smith who was married to a British major in the army. Damn good woman. Has the best collection of Raj stuff I have ever seen.'

I put it in my diary, knowing full well there was little chance I would ever go near the place.

Then speeches and jokes. Everyone had the chance to stand up and tell a joke. It was brave of them to get up, and tell jokes about elocution lessons, Muhammad in heaven, paternity. I managed to avoid joining in – this was getting to be a pattern – and then I slipped off into the night to drive home. Everyone else went to the hotel in Thorpeness.

We played again next morning, another hopeless and embarrassing round, scoring over a hundred. Somehow golf and school did not make it for me, like putting custard on roast beef, and I realised that school had no place in my life; it was simply a moment on a journey that has taken me far away. I mentioned to someone that I represented Vikram Seth (who was at Tonbridge). The man clearly had never heard of Vikram.

'Which house was he?' he asked.

I had no idea. Was it Parkside, I idly wondered, as if it had mattered? I went to the bar and found myself talking to a very elegant man. He wanted to talk about the collapse of language and actually said how much he regretted the loss of the word 'nigger'. What on earth could I say in response to that without seeming a *Guardian* leftie, but I explained to him that I thought it was a very good thing that such words were now deemed inappropriate. He moved on swiftly.

Am I a prig, I wondered? Probably. But the golf was under way. I had six months now till September and the big game. And the Tonbridgians would return, though in a very different manner.

8

The Photocopier Cup

I went back to Scotland. TW and I agreed to play at North Berwick. North Berwick lies east of Edinburgh and the course runs along the coast with some holes almost on the beach. Bracing and rugged. How different from Hammonds End.

Thinking about it, Hammonds End seems primarily to be for the over sixties, which, of course, I am. On one occasion I went into the dining room to have a late lunch and found that my companions were a bridge party of a dozen or so women. They were gracious, and invited me to join in but I know nothing of bridge. Outside, the All Brans (Regulars) were setting off from the thirteenth tee, there must have been thirty elderly men striding, limping and struggling down the fairway veering from one side to another. With their power trolleys ahead of them they looked a formidable bunch.

That particular day was the time of green maintenance, so ahead of them on the fourteenth green were six men led by Neil who runs the course, three machines, one to drive holes into the green to improve the drainage and two to brush the sand across it. Neil had explained to me how the greens were being reworked but little of his skill appeared to be recognised. I asked if he ever addressed the members about how the course was maintained, but he thought there was actually very little interest.

I thought back to the AGM and remembered how many questions about the course were carefully put to one side. No technical staff had been invited, so any such discussion was impossible anyway, but their ruthless exclusion, even of Peter Lane the professional, reminded me of the old days of cricket and the separation of Gentlemen and Players, the amateur and the professional.

As we drove over to the Berwick clubhouse I explained to TW and David, an old friend of his, the details of a new competition which I was due to play later in the month. I had christened it the Photocopier Cup. Justin Hill provides the photocopier in my office in Covent Garden. He decided we needed a better one – a colour copier – and the cost would increase by £50 a quarter. I told him I thought it was too much. Why would a literary agent need a colour copier?

'OK, you play golf don't you?'

'I do.'

'OK let's play for the difference. I'm a member of the Brocket Hall Golf Club, so let's play the match there. I play off twelve.'

He asked me my handicap, seventeen, and he agreed to give me five shots and the wager was made. In effect we were playing for £600. It is Justin's home course.

'You're crazy,' said TW, 'you have no chance. But you

ought to practise competitive golf so let's play for something today.'

There was a lot of joshing around till we settled on the Stapler Cup; it seemed appropriately inconsequential. We set off – it was very windy and I had borrowed clubs but I made a score of eighty-six. Victory. Sort of.

There are two courses at Brocket, the Melbourne and the Palmerston. A few days before the match Justin had rung me just to check the details.

'Do you play in competitions?' he asked.

'Well not many. The Stapler Cup last week,' (I did not mention there were only three of us), 'and once in a championship at Harpenden which was disastrous.'

There was a brief silence.

'So you're not really very competitive – you really ought to play in some competitions.'

I kept quiet.

'See you then on Wednesday at three o'clock on the first hole. Let's play on the Palmerston, it'll be an easier course for you.'

I needed to find out the details of the course and to play it on my own. Secretly. So I booked a round for the Friday before the match. You arrive at a large pair of gates and you have to announce yourself through an intercom.

'Yes, I am booked in at three.'

'Come on in then.'

The gates swung open and I drove past converted barns, and signs to the Auberge du Lac, a posh restaurant, and the Faldo Golf School, before parking and going to present myself at the pro shop. The pro looked me over, asked me for £100, and then gave me a form, which I would then present to the starter who would give me the cards, or rather card as it was only me.

I practised on the range with beautifully stacked balls alongside me before walking up to the first tee. No starter. I waited. I looked out over this big spacious parkland course and the beautiful house, Brocket Hall, dominating the landscape. This was the selfsame house once owned by Lord Brocket who was sent to prison for fraud – he had claimed his Ferraris were vandalised – but it turned out it was a self-inflicted attack, so to speak. Now the course and the house is run by a company. It had, though, a literary connection which I discovered later when I explained what I had been doing that Friday afternoon to the novelist Jim Crace. 'I was born there,' he said. 'If you stand at the front it was in the bedroom at the top on the right. It was Ribbentrop's old bedroom – he was a regular visitor to the house and was a good friend of Lord Brocket, who was interned during the war because of his fascist sympathies.' When I went back I did indeed look, but no plaque yet.

At 2.50 two large men walked up and drove off.

'Played before?' they asked.

'No, but I am playing a match next Wednesday.'

'Terrible course, crap greens,' the larger one said as he went up the fairway.

I waited till they had reached the green. The starter turned up and gave me my card. I drove off.

I had my yardage book (this tells you how far you are

on any point from the green) which had cost a further £10 and a separate notebook so I could scribble comments and tips for Wednesday. The larger man was right, the course is pretty rough and ready but I strode up and down the fairways making notes, looking at the angles of the greens, weighing which club to use on every hole and all this was transcribed in my notebook. This was Justin's home turf after all, but I was prepared and ready.

On the Wednesday I decided to get there early. We were due to play at three o'clock so by then I had practised. No Justin. At 3.20 he drove up in a black Range Rover and leaned out of the window.

'Sorry I'm late, give me a minute or so,' and then to my alarm he came back in a golf buggy.

'Jump in.'

He climbed out and tied my clubs to the back and whisked the trolley alongside us and we sped back to the pro's office so he could sign himself in. I had never been in a buggy before. We started heading in an entirely different direction to get back to the Palmerston. We shot down the path, and Justin turned to me.

'I can't remember what we agreed about which course we should play.'

I now felt my stomach tightening.

'But I thought it would be fun to play the Melbourne.' The other course. The really difficult one.

I did not protest at this point, God knows why. I looked down at my carefully prepared notes but I couldn't admit that I had already been up here. So I stayed silent. And panicked.

We arrived at the first tee and clambered out of the buggy. I could see a lot of water.

'What do you play off?' he asked.

'Seventeen.' I reminded him.

'Where did you get that?'

'At Harpenden.'

'That's probably twenty-two here. Mine is twelve, it would be nine at Harpenden.'

He then explained that in the US, handicaps are weighted for different courses, so I half expected him to suggest he would up my handicap but there was silence on that score. The first hole stood before me. It is a par four sloping violently down to the right to a lake. There is an oak tree on the edge of the lake and the green is about a hundred yards beyond that on the edge of the water. 'We will play off the whites.' All tees have white, yellow and red markers. Reds are for the women and are further up the course making each hole shorter. Yellows are in between but the whites are furthest back, thus making every hole longer and harder.

So there I was on the wrong course, with no notes, no plan and at the mercy of Justin. And white tees, a place I had never been before.

'I like to bet when we play,' he said. 'Let's play for £10 for the first nine, then another £10 for the second and a further £10 for the overall winner.'

I thought we had agreed to play for the extra costs of the photocopier. I mentioned this to him but he brushed that aside and strode up to the first tee. He announced that we would play matchplay, so every hole is a contest. This was not looking good.

'Go for that tree high on the bank and then the ball will run down the slope to settle in front of the green giving you an easy wedge into the green. I'll show you.'

He did it perfectly. Shit. I placed the ball on the tee, took out my three wood, I drove and the ball veered towards the tree, the wrong tree, the one by the water, and settled down by the reeds on the edge of the lake. At least I wasn't in the water, yet. He got into the buggy, and when we reached my ball he told me I was 120 yards from the centre of the green. I realised he was reading it off the screen where the rear mirror normally is. I reached for my eight iron. He drove over to his ball which was perfectly placed. I hooked my shot into the bank to the left of the green and the ball rolled down to the front of the green. He hit his shot on to the green feet from the pin. I overhit my shot on to the green and the ball ran past the pin, I putted back, missed, but holed the next for a five. He putted in, four, and the hole was his.

We went to the second which is a par three driving over the lake. His ball landed on the green ominously close to the pin. I sliced my shot but it was over the lake although it brushed the tree on the right which was hanging over the water. 'That will be in the water,' he said cheerfully. In seconds we were on the green, my head in a swirl. I wasn't sure I could handle the speed of all this. Mercifully my ball was not lost but tucked beneath a tree and I chipped it up on to the green. 'You have a shot here.' He putted and was down for three. My ball was perched feet above and my putt drifted by but I holed the return so the hole was halved. The third is a par five. I took out my driver and the ball went to the left. His was straight. We raced to the ball. It was on a slope and I desperately tried to remember what I should do here.

I vaguely remembered how I was supposed to stand and which club I should use but for safety I went for a five and hit the ball forward to the top of the slope. He hit a three wood to the edge of the green, I hit my third short, then my eight iron nearish to the pin. I had played four shots. His third raced towards the hole then stopped short. He missed a short putt but was down for five. I took two more putts, down in the end for six. I was two down after three holes. The fourth heads back to the river which feeds the lake. It should be a drive, a lay-up to the bank of the river, then an iron over the river to the green but I struggled; the second was too far away from the water leaving me a long shot to the green, but still short of Justin's drive. I closed my eyes and hoped and the ball scrambled over the water. Justin is canny and hit his second over the water to the fairway on the other side. This was much the safest shot with little risk of going into the water and then a straightforward shot to the green. I realised I should have done the same. Too late.

We drove over the bridge and I grabbed two clubs, a wedge and a putter as the buggy headed over to Justin's ball. My ball was sitting in a mess of duck shit below the green. I lurched at it and the ball skidded up the slope of the green before slowly rolling back. I hit it again and the ball got on to the green. Five. Justin was on the green for three and was down for five. The hole was his. That was three down. Things were looking pretty bleak. I had no plan and remembered the advice that I must silence my mind, by now so inflamed it would take a fleet of fire engines to extinguish it.

The fifth is long but I matched his drive though not his second. He was down in five, me in six. Four down. We caught up with three other players – inevitably, given the speed of the buggy, and rushed past them. I wanted to run up a white flag or perhaps hijack the buggy and head back to St Albans. The sixth is a short par three. He drove short of the green; I was away to the left. I chipped on to the green but my putt sped past. I was down for four, he for three. Five down. To be fair he was playing brilliantly but things had to change. He drove the seventh into the bunker. I put my ball safely on the fairway. There is a God. He hacked out; I reached the green with a six iron, and was down in four. He picked up his ball and conceded the hole.

At last I had won a hole. Four down. The eighth is downhill. My driver was safe but my second hit the slope and ran into the rough. His reached the green. He putted safely. His hole. Back to five down. The ninth is a short par three. The tee is high above the green. We both played eight irons to the green. I three-putted, he putted in two. Six down. I had lost £10. He was jolly, as he deserved to be. It was his course, and he was driving the buggy. He was in charge. He was the man. He was winning. And I was fucked.

At this point I admitted to him that I had come up the week before to play the Palmerston course, and I had a bag full of notes as to how to play that course. He laughed. A lot. He really couldn't believe it and started spinning the buggy so much I almost fell out. This seemed a good time to stop so we did and had some coffee.

The tenth and another £10 to play for. We drove safely down the fairway and while I lined up my second he remained in the buggy munching his way through a tube of Pringles. It was hard to concentrate and the ball slid forward into the bunker. Again I struggled forward reaching the green in four. It was his hole. Seven down.

At the eleventh I had a shot, reached the green safely in three and two-putted. He drove off wildly – at last – and with my extra shot I won the hole. I was crawling back. Six down. The twelfth is a par four which I won; five down. The thirteenth is quite short, I out-drove him, hit a wedge to the pin, putted for three, a birdie, my hole. On the back nine I was two up, but overall four down. I was running out of holes to win the match but at last I felt I was making some headway. He was running out of steam but I was a lap behind and out of breath.

The next is a par three, well over 200 yards, I drove into the bunker, losing my nerve, and he reached the green and won the hole. The match was over, five up with four to play. But I told myself I was one up on the back nine. There was still something to play for. The fifteenth doglegs to the left. It was his drive and the ball veered away to the left into the trees. I played safe on to the fairway, his ball was lost, my hole. Two up. The sixteenth is back to the river. I drove high away to the left. Then knocked the ball down safely to the water's edge. His drive was perfect. There is a five iron to the green over the river. He mishit and the ball skidded into the river. I hit mine firmly.

'It's in the reeds on the other side,' he said, 'you should take another.'

'OK.'

I did and the ball reached the green. He dropped another and that too reached the green. We drove over. Joy, my original ball was alongside the green. I putted and won the hole. Three up.

The seventeenth I lost. The eighteenth is a wonderful hole. The tee is high and looks out down over the lake to Brocket Hall.

'OK, let's play double or quits this hole,' said Justin, 'so if I win, I win £20 but if I lose, I lose everything. I'm always up for a gamble.'

I agreed. My drive fell short of a mound in the centre of the fairway, he kept safely left. We drove up and looked for my ball with no success. I searched everywhere but it seemed inconceivable that the ball was lost. I was desperate not to mess up at this late stage so I told him to drive the buggy over to his ball. As soon as he'd gone I could see my ball. It had been underneath the buggy all the time. I wondered. I made a mess of two shots and was left well short of the edge of the lake. The green is on the other side. It looked a long way. It was. Justin knocked his ball forward to the edge; he had an easy shot over the water. It was my shot first. I took a deep breath, and struck the ball. It drifted away to the left but the gods were with me at last and the ball reached the right-hand edge of the green. I was five there so it was not looking good. Justin urged me to take the boat across the lake whereas he would drive the buggy around the bridge further away to the left.

I watched him line up his shot as I pulled the boat across the lake. His shot fell short into the water. I couldn't believe it. He must have been swearing. He walked back to the buggy and got another ball and dropped it. A penalty shot – he was playing five. He hit it. The ball shimmered in the afternoon light as it headed for the green then dipped into the water. Another penalty. The next ball he played did reach the back of the green but it was too late. The hole was mine. I won the back nine by three. Of course I had lost the match. But I didn't care.

We went back to the clubhouse for a drink and some food and Justin explained how the club worked but my mind was elsewhere. I was already thinking about that day in September.

9
Golf School

The days are slipping by and I don't have long before I go back to Aldeburgh. It is a brilliantly sunny day and I am feeling terrifically confident that this might be a day for a stupendous score. I arrive at Harpenden and practise. I hit the practice balls perfectly but the round is pretty terrible as I count up my scores – a lamentable 102, my worst score in the past eighteen months. I arrive home and Heather asks me how I got on. I wonder if I can bluff this out.

'Not too bad,' I mumble as I head for a bath.

'Score?' she asks.

I'm not sure she has really understood the score system so I mention 102.

'That's disastrous,' she says, 'what on earth are you going to do? You know you've only two weeks before you go to Aldeburgh.'

As if I didn't know.

Later that evening I pour a stiff drink.

'Sit down,' says Heather. 'I have a plan for you. You're going to Golf School.'

While I was in the bath Heather had tracked down a golfing school in St Andrews and booked me in for an intensive three days of coaching. It is expensive so she insists I stay in a bed and breakfast. I loathe bed and breakfasts. I hate the faux chumminess of staying in someone else's house even though you don't know them from Adam, they never have a proper bar and being served breakfast by a man in a pinny is just too much. And they use a lot of air fresheners. I explain to Heather that TW has a flat in Edinburgh and he has always said I could use that, as she knows full well. It's not far from Edinburgh to St Andrews and it is free but she is insistent that I stay in St Andrews. I agreed but secretly rang TW to borrow the key.

I took the train on Saturday to Edinburgh. I had a huge golf bag. It was so heavy that at Stevenage I had to find someone at the station to open up the lift. It was simply too heavy for me to drag up the stairs. After a struggle I arrived in Edinburgh and arranged to collect a car. The flat was only round the corner so I wondered if I could deceive Heather by pretending I was in a B & B.

I reached the car-hire desk.

'Sorry sir we are out of cars at this depot – where are you heading?'

'St Andrews.'

'Oh that's no problem we'll take you to our depot at the airport and you'll be well on your way.'

The flat was just round the corner and it was becoming clear my plan to stay in Edinburgh was in trouble. Obviously I would now have to double-back.

The fates were clearly against me but I calculated I had enough time to drive north and at least try to find somewhere, and if it was just too terrible I would then slip out and drive back to Edinburgh and Heather would be none the wiser. I drove north. I gave myself till dark to find somewhere, roughly three hours.

As I headed towards Anstruther I called directory enquiries for the numbers of all the four-star B & Bs in Fife. I started calling them. The Royal Hotel answered. At least it didn't *sound* like a B & B.

'Well sir you will have some trouble finding somewhere – it's Freshers week in St Andrews and all the parents are here delivering their children for the new term.'

I drove on into Anstruther which is eight miles south of St Andrews. I saw the Smugglers Inn, the second recommendation, parked the car and went inside. There was no one to be seen. The dining room looked grim so I went outside and looked up at the windows of what I imagined were the bedrooms. The curtains were pulled casually across the windows – this clearly was not for me so I went across to the car and drove through the town.

There was one B & B which looked nice – I phoned but it was full. I tried one after another, it was getting dark. In the end I drove through a caravan park to a small B & B. I knocked, this must be empty I thought, but no it was full too.

'You could try my sister,' said the owner, 'but she has to leave early, she is doing the Great North Run in Newcastle tomorrow.'

He rang her and then marked her house – Laburnum

Cottage – on the map; she was in a small village south of Anstruther, called Pittenweem.

I headed back south, on the way to Edinburgh of course. It was still early, time if I needed to shoot back to an empty flat in the centre of Edinburgh with Egyptian cotton sheets, and bottles of malt whisky. I drove to Pittenweem and spent some time in the back streets trying to find Laburnum Cottage. Eventually I found it, a bungalow with no Laburnum in sight. I knocked on the door, and the sister answered.

'I'm so sorry, we had a room, yes, but a couple has just come by and taken it – I'm so sorry.'

'That's fine,' I said, perhaps a little too enthusiastically, and hurried back to the car. I was going to the flat. Then I heard a shout.

'OK, I have spoken to my husband – I can make a room up for you.' I knew then there was no way out. Heather had got her way. I was to do time in a B & B after all.

It was a spacious room with a sofa on the left and a large bed. There was a sunken bath and every form of bath stuff – it felt Roman in its extravagance. But I had to share it with the other couple. It was eight o'clock, too early to turn in so I thought I should explore the village. I walked down to the sea and found a pub. It was empty, except for the landlord with a cup of tea in front of him so I ordered a coffee and some whisky and he told me he had been running the pub for over thirty years. He started to tell me the history of the village when an elderly man came in for rum. He explained he was a retired fisherman and had lived in the village all his life. We had a couple of drinks then I made my way back to Laburnum Cottage.

Breakfast at eight, the runner had gone and there were three places set. The couple joined me, farmers from Ayr, whose farm was just above Turnberry. We talked about husbandry, how long to hang beef – three weeks – before I left and headed for St Andrews. So I had survived and actually it hadn't been as bad as I thought.

The academy was just past the Old Course Hotel, a long low building before one reaches the Eden course where I had played with TW earlier in the year. It was a Sunday morning and my lesson was for one o'clock so I drove up the road into St Andrews and parked just by the beach. It was golf I was here for so I went into the Golf Museum from where if you squint a little you can see the eighteenth fairway of the Old Course. I wandered in, a treasure trove for golf loonies, with rows of beautiful wooden golf clubs and I found the original of a print I have at home – *The Blackheath Golfers*, two very dodgy fellows oddly dressed with clubs who look as if they are only dressing up to get into the clubhouse and grab some stuff before disappearing back on to Blackheath.

I was impatient to start, so I went back to the academy and introduced myself to reception.

'George is always late,' they explained.

'Oh well.'

I went and sat down but within minutes George arrived. He took me into the Championship room and explained what would happen over the coming days: three hours of personal instruction every morning then nine holes with him one afternoon. First, however, he had a series of fitness and flexibility tests that he wanted to run through with me. He stressed there were no right answers and he then proceeded to have me standing against the wall, sliding down the wall, twisting my hips like John Travolta in *Grease*, trying to touch my toes – I failed that – but the end result was that he thought I had good mobility in my hips even if my back was a little ropey. He explained he was one of the very few qualified TPI professionals and he would, in due course, send me a set of specific exercises to strengthen my back.

We then had coffee and he asked me if I had any special problems. I explained about the forthcoming Packer Tournament at the end of the week and then set out what I felt my weaknesses were – I could not decide which driver to use, my chipping was erratic, I was terrified of bunkers and my putting had to improve if I had any chance of winning, let alone finishing in the top three.

'Well we have nine hours so let's see what we can do, but on the driver question you should see my friend Pat who runs the technical clinic here.'

As we left the room he popped in to see Pat who agreed to meet me the following morning. I peered through the window to see an array of equipment that seemed more appropriate for a missile-launching site than a golf academy.

We walked down to one of the bays; time for him now to assess my swing. I pulled out my cheap but noble driver and started hitting balls. He watched me for a bit, and then out came the camera and the computer.

'You clearly draw the ball and you have a nice inside-to-outside swing.'

I could relax. I was not going to be dispatched back to Laburnum Cottage as a hopeless case.

'Do you understand ball flight?' George asked.

I was a bit lost here so he went into an elaborate account of swing angles, ball flight and trajectory. He showed me the set-up to do fades and draws. Before long I was beginning to hit a high fade, and I was trying to remember when possibly I would have to hit such a shot, but then I remembered the seventeenth at Hammonds End which had an enormous tree a hundred yards from the tee, yes a high fade would allow me to go round the tree. As I was musing away the camera was whirring, and before long up came the images.

'Here is your posture,' George said.

I looked down to see a tall man stooping towards the ball.

'Look at this angle.'

Suddenly the screen was full of lines tracing my back, the angle of my legs to my bottom, my arm angles. I almost expected a line showing my hair and that it was probably too long.

'The angle on your back is 147. Let me compare you to Tiger Woods.'

Up came a similar image of Woods. Yes he had a much better posture than me. I remembered how else we differed, oh yes he is probably the best golfer the world has ever seen, he is thirty years younger than me and is one of the fittest athletes in the world. I am probably the best golfer in Mount Pleasant and certainly the fittest man living at number 29, but here the comparison ends.

'You hit the ball nicely,' said George, 'but your posture is all wrong. You must give yourself more room, which means you have to stick your bum out more, curve your back and stand further away from the ball. Look at your bum angle against Tiger Woods'.' There was no answer to this, so out came my bum, my back creaked into a new position and I swung towards the ball. A slice, of course, as I struggled to rebalance.

My tutorial was nearly over so we agreed to meet the next morning. I went off to play the short practice course which lay behind the academy. It used to be just a field but now it is a short nine-hole course, each hole being a par three. It is completely flat and I was round in an hour, dropping three shots. It was now five o'clock so I headed for the Ardgovan Hotel, which was part of the package and thankfully not a B & B. I checked in and went down to my room which overlooked a passageway into the kitchen – hardly the eighteenth green on the Old Course. After an hour or so I walked into St Andrews to eat and finished up at the Central, a largish pub in the centre of town. St Andrews is small, effectively two streets running parallel. I sat down, had a pint and found myself chatting to an American who had just brought his daughter across from New York to enrol in the university. He was with his divorced wife but she was out eating separately.

'I just could not bear to be with her tonight, this whole trip has reminded me of why we divorced, and she is so neurotic.'

I explained that I had been married for nearly forty years and our lives had changed so much that it had been like being married half a dozen times.

I was at the academy at 8.30 the next morning. Today was the day of the short game. We went on to the practice area to the left of the long sloping building. There are two greens and four bunkers. Chipping first. George placed a number of balls behind the bunker, with the green just over the lip. He showed me how to do it by bringing the club straight back simply with my arms, not moving the body but using my arms to bring the club back to the ball, so the ball went straight without any spin on it. Good contact was crucial so I needed to be confident in striking the ball. It was not a shot played with the wrists. Often I had tried to flick the ball over the bunker and the usual result was to underhit the ball, the wrists broke, so to speak, and the ball dribbled into the bunker where I was usually trapped for a further two shots. This time my new technique worked and we went back to try to vary the distances. However, I knew the bunker was coming, and after a few moments it came. 'Into the bunker,' he said.

I clambered down and he laid out a number of balls in the sand in a horizontal line parallel to the face of the bunker. He wanted me to play the same shot as he had taught me on the edge of the bunker. He showed me how to do it and ball after ball sailed out. Easy. I took my stance, rather different than Peter had taught me, and I did not shuffle my feet into the sand. The club came back down and the ball flopped into the face of the bunker. I tried it time after time with the ball going in every direction. For the first time at the school I began to feel a mixture of embarrassment and rage. It was now nearly eleven and my excuse to escape from the bunker was that fortunately it was now time to go back into the academy to meet Pat and to investigate my drivers.

We walked through the workshop to the operating table. I laid my cheap and expensive drivers in front of him. He looked at them.

'This is a shit driver,' he said, holding my cheap driver but he then took both back into the workshop to investigate them.

He weighed them, measured their length, the flexibility of the shafts and the angle of the face. I told him I hit the cheap one much more accurately than the expensive branded club. We went back and he asked me simply to hit some drives with my two drivers and he and George huddled over the screen to watch. Behind me there was a small box and it was this box which was to prove so crucial. I hit some drives and my shots with the cheap club were much better.

'Come and look at this,' said Pat.

On the screen were my shots, their trajectory, distance and angle of landing. He had also examined my club head speed and was soon able to tell me why the cheap driver was better. The angle of the face was as it said it was, 9.5, which meant I hit the ball lower, whereas the other driver said it was 10.5 but was actually 12.5 which meant I hit the ball much too high.

'How odd, is this common?' I asked Pat.

'Oh yes, most of the drivers are more angled than they say.'

He explained that most amateurs need a more angled club to get the ball up and so manufacturers take the liberty of simply increasing the angle or loft of the club.

This was just the beginning and before long I had laid in front of me the most systematic analysis – club speed, attack angle, club path, vertical swing plane, horizontal swing plane, face angle of the launch, smash factor, spin rate, spin axis, maximum height, and then with the landing the carry, flight time, landing angle, and the resulting length. The cheap club performed much better. Then Pat explained to me that if I had a better club with the same specifications I could hit the ball a further forty yards, whereas at the moment I was hitting it roughly 210 yards. He explained I needed better ingredients. We went back into the workshop and I asked him if he could make me one.

'Let me see,' he said and disappeared for a moment to make some calls.

Pat came back and said yes he could as he had identified a key shaft which he needed to make the club. He promised to have it ready the next morning. A new club. And one which really would fit my game. At last.

After lunch we went off to play the Kingsbairn course, and it was here that George encouraged me to use my putter from off the green, rather than using my eight iron. We played nine holes then George went off and I continued on my own. It was a beautiful afternoon and I rattled along, in one case scoring a number of pars before the ball started its erratic journey across the fairways. I went back to the hotel having made real progress. Next day I would collect my new driver.

Tuesday was my last day and we went back to the driving range largely to work on my posture. I was gradually learning to push my bottom out and to give myself more room but all I was really waiting for was the driver which was to be ready at eleven. And what a revelation it proved to be. It was a joy to lash the ball into the distance and it kept low with a terrific run. Here technology had proved itself. I was in the hands of a proper craftsman. It was *my* club, suited to my own needs and skills. I was no longer trying to ape Tiger Woods. There was not time to use it on the course as I had to get back home but I could not leave without walking around part of the Old Course.

There is a path which runs along the holes back to the eighteenth green. It is a very simple course. I walked back to the fourteenth and watched a group of golfers with their caddies, moving up the fairway. There were bunkers everywhere. At one stage a rather portly golfer had to lie above the bunker before gingerly lowering himself into it but the shot that came out was exquisite. I reached the seventeenth tee and in front was what used to be the railway sheds but is now part of the Old Course Hotel. The tee is tucked into a corner well to the right. Three men stood on the tee and ball after ball careered into the hotel or into the sheds. A man was posted on the edge of the sheds with a flag. Red disaster, green fine. There were a lot of red flags and after a bit the players gave up and walked round the corner dropping new balls. I felt like jumping over the fence with my new club – let me show you, I would have said – but I turned and got into the car and headed for the airport.

It was time for Aldeburgh. I was a bit worried that all these new things would disrupt my game, but it was a golf school after all, they knew what they were doing. I had new techniques for chipping and I had a new driver and lots of advice about which balls would suit my game. I was ready for the fight. Time to go.

10

The Senior Cup

As I drove east I mulled over everything I'd learnt. George had taught me a number of new techniques and just being with him on the practice area had sharpened my golf in every area. He had told me to keep my elbows tucked in so my swing was much cleaner; my play round the greens was stronger. In three days he'd made me a much better golfer but the real test was still to come.

I decided to stop at Aldeburgh before driving up the coast to Southwold. Once I arrived I couldn't resist a quick round so I paid my green fee and stood on the first tee. The hole stretched before me, hard as a Pakistani cricket pitch. The drive bounced left and I was off. I kept going and scored reasonably well. Later I resumed my journey up the coast feeling quietly optimistic.

I decided to devote Thursday, the day before the championship, to playing two rounds, but I was beginning to wonder if I was becoming too fanatical, so halfway through I gave up and drove home.

Friday. I was up at 6.30 and walked over to the Co-op to buy some croissants. I made Heather a cup of tea and left a croissant by the bed, had my own breakfast and got into the car. As I drove to Aldeburgh my mind wandered back over all those months of preparation and I wondered how Simon would select the pairings. I met him as soon as I drove in and he told me he had paired me with Gerald for the two-ball foursomes in the morning and with John Saner, an old friend from Hertfordshire, in the afternoon. Gerald seemed delighted that we were to play together, as was I.

'It's the Tonbridge Team,' he said.

I thought he was going to get out his old school tie and drape it over his bag, but he didn't.

We started at the tenth. He drove straight and true and we were off to a terrific start. We bogeyed for two points, three points on the eleventh, two on the twelfth then we began to deteriorate and struggled to the turn. I went off the first straight again and we began to recover some lost ground. The other couple consisted of Chris and Ant (who was one of the senior players, a previous winner of the cup). Chris was a trifle wild off the tee whereas Gerald and I were steady. On the second Gerald proceeded to start singing the school song. I hung back, with no memory whatever either of the tune or the words, but Gerald thundered on without accompaniment. We finished the round with a total of thirty-five points which was fine. We were a team. We returned to the clubhouse for lunch.

I was really psyched up by now, desperate to get back to the course. John and I were the sixth couple to go out and we were due to go off at 2.15. I practised my putting and on the dot strode up to the tee.

The first drive with my glorious new driver soared into the sky, bounced, and sped down the fairway. Perfect. My five-iron shot raced into the heart of the green, two putts for a par. Done. I was off to a great start. I reminded myself this was perhaps the most important golf match of my life.

The second runs downhill but you have to drive blindly. The drive went well but my second fell short in the bunker. I decided to stick with my old technique, wiggled my feet into the sand, and gave it a terrific swipe, with my arms, body, whatever I could, and the ball rose from the sand short of the green – but I was out of the bunker at least. I was so elated I then proceeded to push the ball well past the pin, missed the putt back down for six and a single point. It was good to be reminded it was going to be a struggle. Golf is very much a shot-at-a-time game. It can go wrong very quickly; disaster lurks in every bush.

The third is a long par four, over 440 yards, so we had agreed to play it as a five. The drive, God I love this driver, went up the middle, on the green in three, two putts for a five, three points. I knew I needed at least thirty-five points to have a chance so if I played to my handicap I would be OK. Adding it up I had six points in three holes. On the way. On to the fourth, a short par three, both our drives went on to the green, down in three, for three points. Things were looking good. The fifth stretches downhill, a long par four. Drive left, two shots towards the green, but the pin was at the front. I was short and my putter sent the ball past the pin, missed the putt back, down for six, one point.

The sixth is back uphill, a par five with a dogleg to the left. The drive went left, I eased the second up to the dogleg, played a wedge to the green, three putts for a six, two points. John played the hole brilliantly, down in four, to gain five points. The seventh is heading back to the clubhouse with a large bunker at the 200-yard mark which I sailed over. I was beginning to feel a real rush of confidence. My head was under control.

My second with a five iron was short but at least on the green. Two putts for three points. The eighth is short but I was down in four for two points. The ninth tee is high above the fairway, off went the drive, a five to the green, two putts, heaven. I had twenty-one points at the turn. I began to feel dangerously confident.

I got to the tenth where a lot of people were waiting, and there was much talk of the people in front going through with over twenty points. There were still a lot of people behind but there were ominous signs of a build-up. Someone ahead was playing very slowly and the pair directly in front were driving the ball all over the fairway, into the gorse and over the trees. Balls were lost, people returned to the tee to replay their drives – the procedure if you lose a ball – but it meant we waited and waited at the tee, then drove just short of the bunkers, almost 280 yards. A chip, three putts, for two points.

We had to wait again at the next tee. Chris in front drove the ball way to the left and we waited for him to find it, but it was lost and he returned to hit a second drive. By this time Gerald and his partner had caught up with us. I was beginning to lose my concentration as we chatted away. Eventually we drove off and the ball went off to the left, my first bad drive of the day. It skipped over the bunker, and I managed to reach the green in three – we were playing a four as a five – two putts for a five, three points. Again delays. The next drive was OK, a chip then three putts; the putting was beginning to slip, but five shots overall for two points.

At the thirteenth I hooked the ball just short of the gorse on the left, played safely out, mishit the five iron, knocked the next over the green, and was down for six for a single point. I could feel my concentration wobbling. The fourteenth ran alongside Benjamin Britten's house and as if drawn by his music I pulled the ball towards his house. There were people on the green so we had to wait. I played my second towards the green but it was short, then knocked it over the sloping green, three putts for a six, one point. I felt as if I was sheltering under a leaking umbrella which I kept having to patch up.

The fifteenth is a longish par three, and I hit my five iron short, mishit my second, three putts for a five, a point. The sixteenth is a long par four. Thank God there was no wind from the sea which normally makes this hole a nightmare. But by this time the sun was beginning to sink so it was very hard to see where the ball was going. We were beginning to accumulate on the tee. Chris was in front again looking for a lost ball. The leaks were getting worse. Eventually we drove. I sliced to the right, struggled along the fairway to reach the green in four. My energy was slipping away, too many putts no points.

'Come on John, we can do this, two pars to finish off,' I said gamely.

We were trying so hard. The seventeenth is a short three. The day before I had hit five shots into the bunker on the left so my confidence was wobbly, and yes the ball went back into the bunker. I got it out, but short of a tricky green which I misread, down in four, one point. The final hole lay in front. Again a long four which I did in six for a single point. So fourteen for the back nine, making a total of thirty-five. I felt I could have done so much better, but if someone had offered me thirty-five points at the beginning I would have taken it.

We went over to the clubhouse for the prize-giving not knowing anyone else's score. Simon laid out the prizes and we all assembled in front of him. He did the foursomes first and announced the result in reverse order.

'For the third prize, Gerald and David with a score of thirty-five.'

Wow, we walked up to the front to be given six golf balls each. The cheering began, and Gerald was prevented from giving a speech – 'you will speak later' someone shouted from the back and yes there was still the dinner to come.

We then moved to the championship itself. Gerald was way down with a score of twenty-two, one point more than I had last year so I knew I had a chance with a score of thirty-five.

'For third prize David Godwin with thirty-five.'

This was great, and I went up to the table for a second time to get an umbrella. The winners above me were a couple – the husband who had won it the previous year had thirty-nine points, and his wife was the overall winner with forty-four points playing off a handicap of nine. It was a good score. However, there was still one prize to go, the Senior Trophy.

We all sat down. There was still some discussion at the table. Had there been objections, I wondered? Simon stood up.

'The Senior Packer Trophy is won by David Godwin.'

I got up and went to collect the trophy, a magnificent cup set in an elegant wooden base. I held it aloft, for me it was a magical moment. I wanted to offer thanks to all who made the journey with me, but in fact simply slipped the cup under my arm and went back to my seat. It was a victory – not quite the victory I planned for, but a victory nonetheless. I drove home, listening to Handel's *Solomon* and my simple victory swelled to prodigious heights. I showered and returned to the hotel in the centre of Aldeburgh for speeches and dinner. It was a rush, but I got there – and in a suit, much to everyone's surprise; it was, after all, a very special occasion. Speeches, drinks, jokes, toasts, presentations, a truly convivial occasion.

It was wonderful to be part of a community. I could feel the grumpiness and lack of sociability beginning to melt. I thought this book was going to just be about golf, but I was beginning to realise that the whole thing is a lot more complicated. Anyway, my thoughts returned to the golf course; perhaps I could have scored eighty. Maybe I should have done. I thought this was the end of the journey but it turned out not to be.

Epilogue

I didn't break eighty at Aldeburgh. I had done pretty well. I had scored eighty-nine, but the project still nagged at me. I felt the professional coaching hadn't quite worked out for me. I had tried pretty much everything but it had been too undisciplined. I never felt I was following a programme of instruction, which set out the principles of golf and tailored these principles to me, the high handicapper.

I had had lessons in Southwold, which were pretty basic. Then lessons from Peter at Harpenden but he had lost interest in me, and perhaps the loss of momentum had been my fault. I had been to golf school which was intensive but I'm not sure I had really understood what was going on. However, it is easy to find fault with others and perhaps I had been too erratic in seeking easy solutions, jumping from one plan to another and not really concentrating as fully as I should have done. Maybe Peter had detected this, and understood my fickle nature better than I had. I was beginning to understand that my moodiness and lack of sociability were connected, but rather than inspecting my inner psyche any further, I decided it would be easier to continue looking for a golf saviour.

I mentioned this to TW while we were having a drink. He had heard there were some good lessons on YouTube so I went searching there. He was right, and this led me to David Blair. I ordered his DVD and his booklet called *The Secret of Golf*. I watched his short films about The Swing.

He was wonderfully clear and simple and what was so astonishing was that he seemed to address all the problems of a high handicapper. I started practising to his method, and followed his suggestions: I changed my grip slightly but significantly, and for the first time really understood how the golf swing worked and also how crucial the swing is. Obvious really.

However, I needed to know more so I found his number, called and asked him if he would see me if I came up to Glasgow. The next thing I knew I was driving through the dark to catch a flight from Luton to Glasgow to talk golf swings. We spent some time in his garden just swinging a club and he gave me a series of drills to practise at home. He also changed my putting, explaining that the principle of the swing applied to putting as much as to anything else. Basically it involved keeping both arms close to the body and never using the wrists or even the arms. Suddenly I felt this could work so I flew home eager to get going again.

Last winter was full of snow which kept me off the golf course. I wondered if I should join an indoor golf range.

I drove down to Watford to visit the American Golf centre with two levels of golf booths. It was all a bit wild so I thought I would try a London one. I paid my money and was shown a booth. First I had to choose which course I wanted to play. St Andrews. There on the screen in front of me was the view from the first tee. I drove into the screen which calculated where the ball would have landed. I picked up the ball, placed it on the mat and hit the next shot, over the green in the bunker. It is hard to make a mat like a bunker so I went on to the next hole. Putting didn't work either, so although it was good fun it didn't really help my golf.

In April Gerald asked me to play in a charity competition – he was the High Sheriff of Hertfordshire at the time – at a course further west of Harpenden at Ashridge. I drove over on the Friday morning. We all had lunch together, an assortment of men drawn from Gerald's past, some from Aldeburgh, some local, some from his business life, some from school. My heart sank when he told me I was playing in a Tonbridge four. I wondered if I would ever escape school, but the four consisted of the head of Tonbridge golf Tony Monteuuis; Bill, a banker; and John Johnson who was the captain from Aldeburgh. The two best of our four scores counted in the group championship, and there were ten groups. Our own individual scores were also counted.

We started on the tenth, the drive went left but I scrambled the ball on to the green, down for a five against a four. The next hole was a short par three but I sliced the ball into the trees to the right, but made it in five. Not a good start. I drove off last on the twelfth. It is always a bit embarrassing when you play badly. Everyone is kind but tend to look away as you stride up to the ball. I was beginning to feel a bit awkward. However, the drive worked, bouncing down the fairway. The green was slightly raised with a bank running along its left side about 150 yards from where the ball had stopped. Everyone – they had all played the course before – told me to aim at the bank and the ball would run down on to the green. I did as I was told and it worked. The ball finished only a few feet from the hole; I missed the putt and got the next for a four. I felt lucky, and I was. Off I went in a dream, bogeyed the next, birdied the next two, a par five and a par three, parred the seventeenth and then bogeyed the eighteenth.

Suddenly everything came together and we were a team all helping and encouraging one another. I had never played with such camaraderie – this was my school, after all, which I had forgotten about for years and years – and they were willing me on. I didn't bother to count my score but just played as well as I could. On it went, a mixture of pars and bogeys. I made a mistake on the eighth, accidentally tapping the ball as I was practising, but it seemed of no significance. I kept no scores, that was left to Tony. The ninth which we played last is a tricky hole with a blind drive down a slope then a long shot to the green which was raised up, and small. This was not my best hole, scoring a six. We went over to the clubhouse and Tony counted up our team score and gave the cards to Gerald.

We had a drink together on the balcony and as the light faded herds of deer came out of the woods on to the fairways, hundreds of them moving through the misty light.

Gerald came to the front and announced first the group winners in reverse order. The Aldeburgh team came second and we – the Old Tonbridgians – came out first with a score of over a hundred. We were all presented with glass tankards marking the high sheriff's day. It is in front of me as I type.

Then came the individual scores. I came second with forty-two points; John Johnson came first with forty-three playing off an eighteen handicap. He had played brilliantly. I was thrilled and then began pondering what exactly I had done. I took the scorecard back from Tony and slowly added the score. It came to eighty-one and then I remembered that odd nudge of the ball when I was practising my putt on the eighth, which had taken me one shot over; a single small error had robbed me of my goal. But it seemed fine, and actually rather appropriate. No one knew or realised how close I had come, and my achievement had been superseded by a school victory. How deeply ironic it had turned out to be, but my quest was over. Not eighty, but eighty-one. I'll settle for that.

Had I become a better golfer? Yes, would be the simple answer. And it *had* been worth it; all that struggling through the rain, the lessons, the endless practice. I had learnt about the swing, I played more slowly and my putting was better. So I had got better after all, but for me the most significant and surprising thing was that I had achieved it as part of a team. I had learnt that golf is not the solitary sport that I had chosen it to be. My journey had turned out to be a real one after all. I had learnt not to fear clubability as I'm sure it was fear that was stopping me from relaxing and joining in. Golf accommodates all sorts and I must learn to do the same.

I may never become a stalwart of Hammonds End, but I will now be more understanding of those groups struggling and hacking their heroic way down the fairways. In fact I realised then that perhaps togetherness was what really mattered.

I remembered seeing those deer coming out of the trees and I wondered for a moment whether they had known what I had achieved and were there for the celebration. I like to think so.

Acknowledgements

This book would never have been written and my golf would never have improved if Simon de Galleani hadn't kindly invited me to play in the Packer Championship. I owe him a huge thank you. Thank you also to all the golfers who put up with me struggling around the Aldeburgh course, especially Ant Dearden, John Saner and Gerald Corbett. Pauline de Galleani's exceptional hospitality kept us all going during the rounds. I want to thank my most regular partner Bryan Young who, month after month, accompanied me round the Harpenden course. In addition, he and Lesley were generous hosts in Scotland. For the Brocket adventure I want to thank Justin Hill. For support in a crucial round, thank you Tony Monteuuis and the Old Tonbridgians. Peter Lane in Harpenden, the late Brian Allen in Southwold, George Finlayson in St Andrews and David Blair in Glasgow all gave me invaluable professional help. David Davidar made playing in India possible, as did Namita Gokhale and Ravi Purri.

Books need publishers and Rachel Cugnoni took a terrific risk in commissioning this book and I hope she feels it has all worked out in the way she hoped. Matt Phillips and Rowan Yapp have been perfect editors.

My family has played different roles. Simon is an erratic golfer but an excellent writer – he was published before me – and has given me good advice. Sebastian and Hugo have been golf partners of a sort, and great sporting allies. Harriet is not named in these pages but her enthusiasm kept me going when my spirits faltered. The book is dedicated to Heather, rightly so. She has read every word and the result is much stronger for her editorial interventions. More importantly she has supported this project from the very first moment. My one regret is that my mother, who was a very keen golfer, died just before the book was completed.